ENDORSEMENTS

Many books have been written on this subject. *Deep Relief Now* is the *only* one that shows you *how* to receive inner healing quickly and completely!

—SID ROTH
Host, *It's Supernatural*

Deep Relief Now has precious gems of "gut level" tools of release and restoration—it is a must-read for the turbulent times we are navigating through. This book is a brilliantly honest assessment of the what, why, and how-tos to dealing with the burden of the unhealed. Get two copies and give one away!

—MICKEY ROBINSON
Prophetic Destiny International

Deep Relief Now is an essential primer on how to set yourself free from a multitude of hurts, experiences, and relationships that have pursued you and prevented you from enjoying the shalom that is available to you. Whether you are a brand-new convert or not even a convert yet—or you have been in ministry for years—the chances are very strong that there are things holding you back from fulfilling your heavenly assignments. *DRN* is a book that will walk you through the steps to freedom—the shalom given to you in John 14:27. Translated "peace," shalom is much more than that: it means that everything is complete, there is ample provision, no conflict, divine health, and every relationship is in order; it means there is no injustice and no pain!

Deep Relief Now takes you through a process, and on the way you will enjoy the testimonies of Dennis and Jennifer. You will sense their personalities and develop a relationship just by reading their stories. As they weave their ministry for you, the style will hold your attention and hold your hand as you walk through the process. The focus on forgiveness is a major building block of Christian living, often a stumbling block that both Dennis and Jennifer help you to overcome.

My final thought about *DRN* is NTS: it is *none too soon* for you to be digesting this material! Digesting it turns it into action, setting you free.

—WILLIAM J. MORFORD, Shalom Ministries
Author/Translator of *The One New Man Bible*

When it comes to life transformation, the heart of the matter is always a matter of the heart. In this groundbreaking book, Dennis and Dr. Jen Clark provide a timely prescription for what ails the human heart. Though you may have already tried countless other remedies to relieve your emotional pain, don't give up—here's a simple, speedy approach that really works!

—JIM BUCHAN
Crosslink Ministries

Deep Relief **Now**

DESTINY IMAGE BOOKS
BY DENNIS AND JENNIFER CLARK

Live Free

Deep Relief **Now**

Healed,
Free,
Whole

Dennis & Dr. Jen Clark

DESTINY IMAGE® PUBLISHERS, INC.

P.O. Box 310, Shippensburg, PA 17257-0310

"Promoting Inspired Lives."

This book and all other Destiny Image, Revival Press, MercyPlace, Fresh Bread, Destiny Image Fiction, and Treasure House books are available at Christian bookstores and distributors worldwide.

For a U.S. bookstore nearest you, call 1-800-722-6774.

For more information on foreign distributors, call 717-532-3040.

Reach us on the Internet: www.destinyimage.com.

ISBN 13 TP: 978-0-7684-0414-2

ISBN 13 Ebook: 978-0-7684-0415-9

For Worldwide Distribution, Printed in the U.S.A.

5 6 7 8 / 18 17 16

DEDICATION

We dedicate this book to Cliff and Stina Coon, Molly Tarr, Vicky Rose, Barbara Price, and Kim Flint. Thank you for your unwavering support, your friendship, and encouragement throughout the years. You stood with us and believed. We also thank Jason Clark and Rich Myers for your passion and commitment. You have all caught the vision and made it your own.

CONTENTS

WHY YOU NEED THIS BOOK

Hurting People Can Be Healed:

A Word from Dennis

People are hurting. As a pastor I see it every day. But one doesn't have to be a pastor or possess a unique gift of discernment to understand that people are hurting. The evidence is everywhere we look. Tabloids at the grocery store describe in large fonts how celebrities are experiencing meltdowns in their marriages, children, careers, sobriety, and even their own sanity. They're rich and famous and seem to "have it all," yet they are hurting deep inside.

You don't have to be a celebrity to experience emotional pain. It happens to all of us—and I mean *all* of us. Fortunately, we don't have the paparazzi following us around with their cameras, documenting our shortcomings, pains, and fears. But God sees our pain, and He wants to help us in the midst of it. In fact, He longs to help us out of it. And that's why Jen and I wrote this book.

This is not just another book on counseling or self-help. As you can see from the title, we are making a very bold and audacious claim. No matter how deep or longstanding your pain may be, if you follow the simple solutions offered in this book, you can experience deep relief right now—you don't have to wait another day.

Perhaps you've lost hope in traditional counseling and therapy—so have we! But in contrast to the largely ineffective methodology you may have tried in the past, we've discovered an approach that can provide deep relief for your deepest hurts.

What do we mean by this? If you've received no lasting relief despite spending thousands of dollars on traditional forms of psychotherapy, then you're not alone. Perhaps you feel like the woman with the issue of blood described in the Bible: *"a long succession of physicians had treated her, and treated her badly, taking all her money and leaving her worse off than before"* (Mark 5:26 MSG). The proven method presented in this book has brought true and lasting relief to countless people—and it can provide relief to you as well.

Here are just a few testimonies of people who have found deep relief in the midst of their pain. One person told us after experiencing deep relief now: "I carried shame around for my entire life, but I paid it no more attention than to my shadow. I simply didn't realize what it was and how much it was coloring my world. After using the Clarks' how-to tools, I feel different without even trying. One of the tangible differences I notice is that I now can look people in the eye—something I didn't realize I had difficulty doing before. Overall, I feel much freer, cleaner, and more emotionally whole than I ever have before."

Another individual writes, "Through the how-to tools I learned from Dennis and Dr. Jen, I was completely delivered and healed from a spirit of rejection—something that had plagued me my whole life. Instead of always feeling on the outside of things, I now feel a part of other people's lives. The change is amazing!"

"I was always fearful—*very* fearful," writes another. "But deciding to try the Clarks' approach, I dropped down and let it go. *Whoosh*...the fear was gone! This truly was truly deep relief now. What ten years of counseling couldn't do, God did through DRN in just minutes."[1]

If God did it for these people, then He surely can do it for each and every one of us.

But the sad truth is that many people don't believe it's possible to actually have their deepest hurts healed. So what's the next best thing? Medication! Instead of seeking deep relief, they settle for solutions that merely mask the symptoms. And let's be honest: modern pharmaceuticals often *do* provide a measure of relief. Many people are able to carry out relatively normal lives by numbing their pain and elevating their mood through seemingly miraculous medications. But ask yourself this: Would you rather relieve your headaches through endlessly popping Advil, or would you rather eliminate the underlying conditions that are causing your headaches in the first place? This book is about good news: you can experience deep and lasting relief of your underlying emotional hurts.

The message communicated by most of the professional counseling community today sounds a lot like some medical professionals I've met: "I can't really heal you, but if you come in for regular appointments over the course of many years, I can at least make your pain manageable." This model of therapy makes patients even more dependent on the therapist, never fully able to stand on their own two feet. However, deep relief now means just what it says...you can actually experience deep relief, and you can experience it right now.

Before we go on to share how this all works and how it is applied to our life, Dr. Jen (my lovely wife) and I want to share some of our story of experiencing this amazing discovery for ourselves. But before we do that, Dr. Jen wants to say a few words.

Something that Works:

A Word from Dr. Jen

Dennis and I wrote this book not just to tell you our story, but to pave the way for God to break into *your* story. We want to give you something that works—something that will bring deep relief from the pain and frustration you're currently experiencing. Why do we want to share deep relief now (DRN) with you? Because we know you don't have to remain in inner turmoil and distress. You've probably already tried to address your pain in many different ways, so we understand if you're skeptical that DRN can help. But that's why I wanted to share my own story. Despite all my degrees, diplomas, and research, my inner hurts still remained. Yet the simple truths of DRN brought me internal freedom I never thought possible.

What God taught to Dennis and me, you can learn also. If you follow the easy-to-grasp process, you can have the same results we obtained. After seeing thousands of lives touched, we are confident that no pain is too severe or too deep for the Lord to relieve, quickly and permanently.

Dennis learned the concepts of deep relief now over the course of 35 years of experience as a pastor and counselor. Now we're able to put it into a simple format that works for anyone, at any age, and at any time. That means it can work for you, today, in the midst of whatever it is you're going through.

DRN can be taken as far as you want to go with it. Whether you just want to quickly deal with a few wounds or receive a total life transformation like me, these principles are powerful, life-changing tools. And it's our prayer that, as God uses DRN to change your own life, you will want to help others as well. One individual told us after receiving relief from years of pain, "DRN has permanently changed my life, and I've seen it change other people as well. The principles are universal, able to help people anywhere on the planet. I'm excited about using DRN to help other people find deep and lasting relief and transformation."

Don't just take my word, but listen to what Lou, a pastor, has to say: "The DRN approach really works. There are tangible results. I've seen it work pretty much 100 percent of the time. And I think the reason it has results is because it's based on a relationship with the Lord. Also, it facilitates a supernatural transaction, resulting in a truly supernatural exchange. This is such a joy in contrast to trying to do everything in our own intellect. As a pastor, I now have new tools to equip my people to allow the Lord to do the work in them."

So what are you waiting for? You can experience deep relief from your emotional pain—and you can experience it now, at this very moment. Deep relief now really works, and works quickly.

ENDNOTE

1.   Not only are there many such testimonies contained throughout this book, but to read more stories like the ones in this chapter, turn to the Appendix: More Testimonies.

Part One

DISCOVERING DEEP RELIEF NOW

Chapter 1

HITTING BOTTOM, FINDING FORGIVENESS

By Dennis

Confessions of a Troubled Soul

I was raised as a Catholic and went to parochial school from kindergarten through second grade. As a young Catholic, I struggled with the whole concept of confession of sins and forgiveness. Between visits to the confessional, I found myself tormented by the guilt of my sins and apparent inability to change my behavior.

Before I even made it home from the confessional, I found myself plagued by unkind, selfish, or lustful thoughts, and this led me to an inevitable conclusion: the only way I could ever make it into heaven was to be hit by a car as soon as I had confessed.

I was also troubled by the realization that I never told the whole truth in the confessional. Full honesty would cause me to undergo too much penance, so I did everything possible to sugarcoat my sins. However, this didn't really work either. I knew that if I received forgiveness, it would be based on an incomplete accounting of my misdeeds.

The result of this never-ending cycle was that, although I craved forgiveness, I never really experienced it. Having a true relationship with God in this life seemed impossible, let alone making it through the pearly gates after I died.

Looking for Relief

Everyone is looking for relief—deep relief—from some kind of inner torment or dysfunction. People pursue different remedies to "medicate their pain," but the result is always the same: a downward spiral of even greater pain and emptiness. In my case, I looked to drugs to give me relief and numb my emotional agony. It's ironic that people describe drugs as giving them a "high," because they usually end up, like me, hitting rock bottom.

By this time I had a wife and infant son, and I had to rely on welfare to support our family. My addictions, bad attitudes, and utter helplessness without God had crippled my ability to be the provider God intended.

At last, I reached my "pigpen moment" (see Luke 15:15-16) —our baby was sick and needed medicine. I had been given a Medicaid prescription, but it was tossed into the trash by accident. In desperation, I found myself standing in a dumpster, digging through the trash so our son could have the medicine he so desperately needed. Friends and acquaintances drove by honking and waving as they recognized me standing red-faced in the dumpster. It was a moment of total humiliation, but also a much-needed wake-up call.

Born Again

Many years later, several Christians told me I'd been so wild they thought it was useless to bother even praying for my salvation. They explained that they had focused their prayers on people who seemed to have more of a chance of getting saved. However, someone must have been praying for me, because at 29 I finally experienced God's gift of salvation and was born again during a Christian television program.

Within the first year, I had such unusual and dramatic spiritual experiences that I was thrown onto the local Christian television circuit to share my testimony. Even though I was a complete novice in the Christian life, people marveled at how God had so rapidly transformed me.

Although the Lord taught me many wonderful things in those early days as a new convert, I particularly fell in love with the concept of forgiveness. Not only did I have my own struggles with forgiveness at the confessional, but my family line was also known for unforgiveness. I remembered hearing my mother once say with great pride, "I *never* forgive and I *never* forget!"

My mother's sister was the exact same way. When I was just a teen, I didn't want to dance with my cousin because she was taller than me. When my mother asked why I refused to dance with her at a particular event, I answered, "She's just too big!" Well, my mother made the mistake of sharing my explanation with her sister, saying I thought her daughter was too big to dance with. Because of this seemingly insignificant incident, my aunt was so offended that the two sisters didn't speak to one another for 14 years after that.

What a silly mess it all was. My mom's sister was offended, and my mom was offended that her sister was offended. And all of this because of a misunderstood statement by a teen about not dancing with his cousin because she was taller than he.

A Forgiveness Lifestyle

Jesus paid a tremendous price to give His greatest gift to mankind: the gift of forgiveness. This amazing gift is our ticket to freedom, the bringer of peace, the heart healer, and the balm for strained relationships. Without Jesus paying the price for forgiveness, we would be stuck in our sins, not to mention the great emotional pain that accompanies them.

To my great surprise and relief, no more trips to the confessional were necessary to provide my forgiveness. I learned from 1 John 1:9 and other passages that I could go directly to Jesus and receive forgiveness—any time, any place. John reminds us, *"If we confess our sins, He is faithful and just to forgive us our sins and to cleanse us from all unrighteousness."*

I made up my mind that I was going to live a lifestyle of forgiveness. I learned to immediately receive forgiveness when I sinned and extend forgiveness when people wronged me. And I also discovered that whenever I felt negative emotions, my peace could be restored through receiving God's forgiveness or deciding to forgive Him, myself, or others.[1] I didn't have to go another moment without His presence accompanying me.

Although I fell in love with the whole concept of forgiveness, I initially encountered one significant problem when I began to put it into practice. I found that I had so many impure thoughts, bad attitudes, and offenses that I was either forgiving or receiving forgiveness all day long. I didn't have time for anything else. Forgiveness was truly fantastic, but it was taking up all my time. I wondered how I could ever get any work done and still manage to live in forgiveness, staying aware of the flow of His presence.

Despite this concern, I simply made up my mind that I was going to stick with this anyhow.

Fortunately, things soon got better. I was relieved to discover that the times between my "forgiveness episodes" were getting farther and farther apart. The practice of forgiveness was actually changing me on the inside, gradually transforming my thoughts, attitudes, and actions.

Knowing God

Growing up on the tough streets of Chicago, I had learned the art of scowling to intimidate people and causing them to keep their distance. This "street sense" was simply a matter of self-preservation. Like Chicago gang members, I had begun to use anger as a wall of defense.

But now my countenance was radically different. Instead of anger, most of the time I felt and projected intense joy. In fact, I smiled so much that I earned the nickname "Smiley." Thankfully, I was living in Pennsylvania at that point, because my beaming smiles would have gotten me beaten up in Chicago.

One of the early lessons I learned was that I could perceive God's presence when I spent time with Him. My prayer times weren't focused on asking God for things, although that is valid during prayer, but simply on enjoying my relationship with Him. I discovered that if I simply pursued God, He gave me everything else I needed without ever asking for it (see Matt. 6:33). This was much more than just following a method or philosophy—I was communing with a real Person.

I also found that just as in a relationship with another human being, the more time I spent with the Lord, the better I got to know Him. I began to understand His likes and dislikes, the inner sound of His voice, the gentle touch of His love and pleasure, and the nuances of His personality. Paul perfectly described the long-ings of my heart to know and commune with God in Philippians 3:10 (AMP):

> *[For my determined purpose is] that I may know Him [that I may progressively become more deeply and intimately acquainted with Him, perceiving and recognizing and understanding the wonders of His Person more strongly and more clearly]...*

Paul's words here are not to be taken as just the experience of an elite group of super-spiritual Christians. Rather, they are meant to be the normal life of every believer—pressing on each day to better know the Lord through deep intimacy and commu-nion with Him.

The School of the Spirit

One of the most important lessons I learned in my early days as a Christian was the value of discernment. Through the Scriptures and the Holy Spirit, God was revealing Himself to me as my loving heavenly Father. I discovered that there were numerous counterfeits of God's presence, and I needed an abil-ity to discern which spiritual experiences were authentic and which were not.

People responsible for detecting counterfeit money are trained to discern what real currency looks like, and I found that the same principle applies to the spiritual realm as well. They are trained to spot counterfeit bills by looking at and feeling the real thing so much they can detect when something is wrong. I likewise set my heart on knowing God's loving nature so intimately that I wouldn't be fooled by cheap imitations.

I learned that the nature of God is always loving, patient, and pure. Even when we need His rod of correction, we can sense that all of heaven's love is behind it. I soon became so acclimated to a loving, heavenly environment that I developed an antipathy for anything that blocked my inner sense of God's presence. The more I became acquainted with the reality of God, the more I felt an aversion to any negative emotion that disturbed my peace with Him. And the Lord taught me that forgiveness always brought me back to an amazing sense of peace.

God was personally taking me to the school of the Holy Spirit each day, instructing me in the intimate language and unique whisperings of the Spirit. I found that when the Lord awakened me at night to pray, it felt as gentle as the brush of a feather across my cheek. In time I also learned to be obedient even to these gentle promptings.

Surprising Lessons

Some of the Holy Spirit's lessons completely surprised me. For example, it was puzzling at first that when the Lord quickened a verse of Scripture and I began talking to Him about it, the Spirit's anointing diminished. God explained to me, "You don't have anything worthwhile to say unless you first have heard something."

Isaiah 50:4 (AMP) teaches this very thing—that if we're going to speak a timely word to someone, we must first learn to hear God's voice as one who is taught:

> *[The Servant of God says] The Lord God has given Me the tongue of a disciple and of one who is taught, that I should know how to speak a word in season to him who is weary. He wakens Me morning by*

morning, He wakens My ear to hear as a disciple [as one who is taught].

I also learned that when God speaks, we need to truly absorb His words and make them a reality in our lives. If we're too eager to share what we've heard, our message is only information, not revelation. This means we must learn how to listen *and* wait in the presence of the Lord. Isaiah communicates this promise to us when he says, *"Those who wait on the Lord shall renew their strength; they shall mount up with wings like eagles, they shall run and not be weary, they shall walk and not faint"* (Isa. 40:31).

I discovered that one of the great benefits of waiting on the Lord was that I became aware of God's constant presence in my life, and I paid attention when I felt any change or diminishing of the anointing. Whenever I sensed any change at all, I asked questions like, "God, did I do or say something wrong?" or "Lord, I felt a quickening in my spirit when I thought about going to the bookstore. Does that mean You want me to go there?" I loved experiencing His presence in that way. And I became increasingly sensitive to avoid any thought, word, or action that would hinder my relationship with Him.

It wasn't enough to just experience God during my prayer times (as wonderful and life-giving as that was), but I wanted to take the same sense of His presence that I felt in my prayer time with me all day long. I learned that I experienced His presence through different supernatural "emotions"—sometimes as a deep peace, and at other times as unspeakable joy. But there was always an awareness of His awesome holiness and love. I was learning to enjoy the fruit of the Spirit as a daily reality.

Learning from Brother Lawrence

Although God had put me in His personalized school of the Holy Spirit, He also sent me helpful mentors at various points along my journey. Some of these were believers who modeled the Christian life for me, but others were great men and women of God who "mentored" me through their writings or biographies, long after they were gone.

Brother Lawrence, who lived from 1614 to 1691, was a monk in a Carmelite monastery in Paris. After he died, his letters were compiled into a book called *The Practice of the Presence of God.* It became one of the most popular Christian books of all time, among both Catholics and Protestants alike. Throughout the centuries, Brother Lawrence has been often quoted by such great Christian leaders as John Wesley and A. W. Tozer.

This humble monk, who lived hundreds of years ago, became a tremendous example for me. He sought to spend his entire life in unceasing adoration and communion with God in every thought he had, word he spoke, and action he performed. Loving God became the central theme and purpose of his life. Even while engaging in the mundane chores and activities of life, Brother Lawrence sought to glorify God and experience His presence. He didn't try to accomplish anything great—he simply sought to live in love.

Brother Lawrence stood out among his peers because of his Christlike example. He gained a reputation for living in such intimacy with God that he constantly experienced deep and profound peace. For him, prayer wasn't just something to cross off a to-do list each morning. Instead of being something he did, prayer was Someone he loved. Brother Lawrence modeled the kind of life I craved, a life of prayer without ceasing (see 1 Thess. 5:17).

Discerning the Spiritual Atmosphere

Have you ever noticed how easy it is to be influenced by the unpleasant environments around you? Perhaps we've felt nervous while watching another person who was nervous when speaking before a crowd. Or maybe we've felt ourselves getting angry when surrounded by angry people. This experience of picking up the spiritual environment around us is actually a form of discernment. It's an example of being sensitive to the atmosphere of the world around us. If we stay peaceful inside, even though we discern a negative atmosphere around us, we don't have to let it cause us to lose our peace.

As I became more acclimated to experiencing God's loving nature, I began to fiercely dislike anything that interrupted my peace. And I found that while I honed my awareness of the presence of God, I also developed a great sensitivity to other people. When they were nervous, angry, or hurting, I was able to pick up their emotions quite easily.

In my early days as a believer, however, I still had plenty of hurts, wounds, and rejections. Because of this, it often triggered my own pain and insecurities when I felt the pain of others. So I begged the Lord to take away this new sensitivity: "Lord, I have way too much of my own pain. I certainly don't want to feel the pain of others!"

A pivotal moment occurred during the first year after my conversion. I had been asked to share my testimony at a small meeting one evening. But when I went up on the stage to speak, out of the blue I was hit by an overwhelming wave of fear and shame. I was so gripped by these toxic emotions that I couldn't say a word. I just walked off the platform, and the worship leader filled in the gap and gave her testimony instead. What a humiliating turn of events it was. I loved Jesus with all my heart, and was having rich experiences with Him in prayer. But something was wrong with me.

As soon as I got home, I fell on my knees in prayer and cried out, "Lord, I don't understand what happened. Where did this come from?" Instantly, I saw myself as a nine-year-old boy with clenched fists, hating himself for being a bed-wetter. Two decades removed from that painful time in my life, I felt the hatred and shame just as if it happened yesterday. I had always known it was wrong to hate other people, but now I was seeing how wrong and harmful it was to hate myself.

As I humbled myself in prayer, I experienced the Lord washing away my feelings of shame and removing the self-hatred from my heart through receiving forgiveness. As soon as I was cleansed of these negative emotions, my heart was flooded with the incredible love and peace of God once again.

I realized I had learned a profound secret, important not only for my own Christian life but for countless others who needed similar hope and healing. Starting with this pivotal incident, the Lord began to show me how bad emotions interrupt our ability to practice His presence. As I learned to deal with these negative emotions, I found that I was able to connect with the love nature of God once again.

Somehow it surprised me that whenever I invited God to come and touch an area in my heart, He really showed up and did it. I discovered that Bible principles truly work, and Jesus does what He says He will do. He is always faithful to His promises, yesterday, today, and forever. God is always willing to save and He is always willing to sanctify.

We often tell lost people they should open the door of their heart to Jesus in order to receive His salvation, and that is true.

But now I was discovering I could choose to continuously open my heart to Him. Jesus said, *"Behold, I stand at the door and knock. If anyone hears My voice and opens the door, I will come in to him and dine with him, and he with Me"* (Rev. 3:20). Of course, in the original context of this passage, Jesus is speaking to Christians, not unbelievers like is so often assumed. His offer of intimacy and freedom is made to anyone who hears His voice, and that is good news for you and for me.[2]

As the Lord taught me to walk in forgiveness and cherish His love and peace, it became apparent that this must become a way of life for me, not just a series of random events. I had been equipped with some powerful "God-tools"—practical how-tos for walking moment by moment in the Lord's presence. But now I learned to apply those tools in my daily life and would one day begin to teach these same principles to others.

These foundational experiences formed the basis for deep relief now. In the following chapters, you'll learn how to begin applying these secrets in your own life. As your life begins to radiate new peace and joy, get ready for people to ask what has happened to you. When they ask, "Where did you learn this?" make sure to buy them a copy of this book.

But first, please allow Jen and me to explain more of our stories so you understand the principles in the context of our relationship with the Lord. Principles without relationship only turn into form, and having the form without the power doesn't help anyone.

ENDNOTES

1. This is not to say that God sins or needs to ask for our forgiveness, but rather that we are often offended or hurt with Him for allowing certain circumstances into our lives—people sinning against us, traumas, etc. It is as times like these we need to extend forgiveness to God, not to pardon Him, but to release the pain we hold in our heart.

2. Also, Jesus addressed this passage to a specific church. But a "church" is an assembly of believers who must open their hearts to Jesus in order for Him to come in.

Chapter 2

A COUNSELOR IN NEED OF HEALING

By Dr. Jen

The Day that Changed Everything

We were two strangers—a pastor named Dennis and me, a Christian psychologist—traveling from different parts of the country to attend a conference in Jacksonville, Florida. I had been to plenty of conferences before, but none of them changed my life quite like this one.

During one of the sessions, a young woman named Amanda suddenly had an emotional meltdown. Completely freaking out, she collapsed onto the floor, weeping uncontrollably. And nobody helped her. Here we were at a Christian conference, and nobody did anything to relieve her distress. Instead, everyone simply froze in their tracks, staring in shock as the tormented young woman writhed on the carpet.

As a psychologist, I *wanted* to help her, but what could I offer her? As I quickly took mental inventory of the psychological tools in my toolkit, I thought to myself, "Five or ten years of counseling *might* give her some relief! But what about now? Can anything be done to relieve Amanda's distress at that very moment?"

After a brief moment of hesitation, a pastor came over and calmly knelt beside the hysterical woman. Step by step, he began to coach her, and Amanda's intense emotional pain was quickly and easily transformed into deep peace. It was an amazing scene. In less than ten minutes, the distraught young woman was up on her feet, smiling and calm, testifying that her emotional pain was gone. Yes, it was completely gone!

As a psychologist, this was a mind-blowing experience for me. I had all sorts of education, training, and degrees in how to give people relief from their emotional pain, but I had never seen anything like this. While my approach was well meaning and theoretically sound, I was struck that this pastor's approach really worked. It not only brought deep relief, but it brought it *fast*. Astounded, I exclaimed to myself, "This is huge!" In a flash, I saw what such rapid and thorough emotional healing could mean to a world full of hurting people.

My life has never been the same since that day when I saw a young woman's life transformed in mere moments. That's also the day I met Dennis—the pastor, who is now my husband—and he started teaching me about the revolutionary tool we call deep relief now (DRN).

There Had to Be More

Before that pivotal day in Jacksonville, I had become very disillusioned in my role as a Christian counselor. With all my heart I wanted to see people find real relief from their problems. Yet most of my clients and friends either made progress that was extremely slow, or they seemed to make no progress at all.

One medical doctor told me of his frustration in trying to help people in his church overcome various addictions. He said, "I know the Bible says believers are supposed to be new creations in Christ, but I see the same old never-ending issues." Another counselor shared her conclusion that a person had to be pretty well adjusted at the time of salvation, or else they were most likely too wounded to ever be of much use in Christian ministry.

Despite seeing these discouraging results, I clung to the hope that somewhere there must be a solution that actually brought people emotional healing in a deep and lasting way. Like a relentless investigative reporter, I went on a personal quest to discover some keys the counseling community had perhaps overlooked.

I studied. I prayed. I interviewed counselors who were considered "experts." From psychoanalysis to Christian inner healing and deliverance, I didn't want to leave any stone unturned in my pursuit. I investigated the role of medication, support groups, and altar calls—but still I felt like I was only scratching the surface in trying to solve people's deep-seated emotional and behavioral problems.

What About You?

Perhaps you've experienced this same frustration in trying to find relief for yourself or the people you love. Maybe you feel as though you've tried everything, yet the inner turmoil still remains. Before we go on to examine and experience deep relief now, I want to encourage you to do an honest personal assessment of your need for emotional healing. Ask yourself questions like these:

- Have I ever felt out of control and unable to stop myself from doing some kind of undesirable behavior?

- Do I struggle with unrelenting fear, emotional pain, or feelings of rejection or inferiority?

- Have I tried a variety of remedies—spiritual or secular, self-help or professional—with only limited relief?

- Have I reached the point where I'm no longer expecting to get any better, but just struggling to hold on?

Perhaps you are one of millions of people in our country who have sought help from a professional counselor. If so, I applaud you for seeking solutions to your problems. However, you need to be honest with yourself at this point if true change is to occur in the future. As Dr. Phil likes to ask people, "How's that workin' for you?"

If you are like countless other people, then after years of counseling, psychotherapy, or support groups, your pain remains. Medication has given you partial relief, but you suspect that it's just covering up the symptoms, not bringing you actual healing deep in your soul. The bottom line is that you've spent thousands of dollars on remedies that haven't really worked. Sure, you feel better for a short time, but no lasting results come from it.

If you've experienced this frustration in your life or seen it in the lives of your loved ones, isn't it time for a change? I want to pull back the curtain on my own struggles and share more about how God transformed Dennis and me through the discovery of deep relief now.

Yes, Even Counselors Need Deep Relief

Needless to say, many people that become counselors don't have it all together in their own lives. If they say they do, then just ask their spouse or children if they are truly healed of all their emotional issues. I can almost bet that 100 percent of those you ask will tell you that they don't have it anywhere near all together.

People often go into psychology or counseling in an attempt to find solutions for their own inner pain. Hopefully, their pain has also caused them to have compassion for others, but that doesn't mean their own struggles have been resolved or somehow ceased to exist. Usually they just learn to cope with life's challenges and maintain their outward composure in spite of their hidden emotional turmoil.

This is what my life as a psychologist was like when I attended the conference in Jacksonville. Most of the time I managed to present an appearance of professional confidence and decorum, but beneath the surface I was experiencing hidden torment. Despite all my psychological training, I was still trapped in my past—bound by secret hurts, wounds, fears, anger, and shame.

Yes, my training had given me lots of tools for emotional healing, but there was just one problem: the tools were largely ineffective. Instead of bringing me actual transformation and healing, these tools caused me to push my issues even deeper.

However, when God used Dennis to show me the amazing principles of deep relief now, I didn't have to bury or "stuff" my issues any longer. In a remarkably short period of time, my internal conflict vanished. For the first time in years, I could be childlike without being childish, laugh without crying on the inside, express my heart without being demanding or controlling, and deal with conflicts without flying into emotional outbursts.

When I realized the awesome depths of my transformation, I felt like shouting at the top of my lungs, "Free at last! Free at last! Thank God Almighty, I'm free at last!"

How Did I Get These Hang-Ups?

Those who meet me today often conclude that I've always had a pretty carefree life. So they're puzzled when I describe my hidden inner turmoil before meeting Dennis and finding out about deep relief now. Like many of us, I've discovered life isn't always easy. So let me share some more of my own story.

Born and bred in Tallahassee, Florida, I was a headstrong child with a strong-willed father. We frequently butted heads, and I found myself angry at his control and angry with myself for not being assertive enough to get my own way.

As a result of the personality clashes with my dad, I internalized a lot of resentment and pain. Feeling intimidated and fearful, I was well behaved on the outside, but on the inside there was a rebel waiting to get out. Fortunately, I concentrated on my schoolwork and avoided getting in with the wrong crowd. My dad saw my good grades and strong work ethic, and he concluded my only acceptable career options were to become a doctor or an attorney.

Well, I decided I wanted to be a psychologist instead. My father considered this a terrible choice and told me so: "That's no better than becoming a witch doctor!" He was not for it, to say the least.

Marriage, Children...and Widowed

When I was just 21 years old, I married a physician named George and moved to the small town of Waycross, Georgia. Over the next few years, I had two children, did some mountain climbing, went to graduate school, and got saved.

Having Christ now in my life was a great adventure, and I was thrilled by the changes He brought. However, George was running away from God, and he was distressed by my decision to follow Christ. He thought I must have thrown my brains out the window in order to "believe all that Bible stuff."

Although persecution can strengthen our faith and build our character, it can also rip our heart to shreds when a person we love says harsh words to us and ridicules our relationship with the Lord. I found that the anger and fear of my childhood were compounded by a new level of pain and sorrow.

George's anger and rejection caused me to suffer greatly. But somehow the Lord showed me that this resentment was not really toward me, but toward Him. The pain was unbearable at times. Even though I shed many tears, my psychology training helped me understand my "issues" and learn to cope with my situation. Years later, I would learn that Jesus wants us not just to cope with life but to actually enjoy it. He said, *"I came that they may have and enjoy life"* (John 10:10 AMP).

You see, until I learned that it was possible to have deep relief from our hurtful feelings, coping was the best outcome my psychology studies could offer. Superficial relief, after all, was better than no relief at all. At least it meant I had moments of relief, or it least it felt like I did.

New challenges arose in 1993, however, when my husband died of lymphoma. George had gone through a traumatic two-year battle but the cancer eventually won. Thankfully, my pastor had driven to the hospital in Atlanta and led George to the Lord just six days before his death. God was working in the midst of my pain.

After my husband died, I was determined not to let myself get caught up in the grief and fear of widowhood, because I needed to focus on surviving and taking care of my two children. My son, John, was already away in college, but my daughter, Allison, was just nine years old when her dad passed away.

My coping mechanisms often found themselves at the breaking point. Despite my best attempts to ignore the emotional turmoil in my heart, it was still very much there. Stuffed under the surface, it had an inconvenient way of popping up and overwhelming me from time to time.

Rough Times

Between 1993 and 1997, my kids and I went through some really difficult times. I commuted a total of three hours a day to and from work. Every day was a tiring journey through back roads and small towns. This long commute meant leaving home in the dark and arriving home when it was dark once again.

That sort of schedule was terribly difficult, both on me and on John and Allison. After three years, I was physically and emotionally exhausted and realized something had to change. Although I didn't really know how things could possibly change, I clearly couldn't keep up this grueling schedule for much longer.

After being widowed, I went almost five years without going on any dates. I reasoned that if God had another husband for me, it wouldn't be any problem for Him to bring someone into my life. I told my friends, "Instead of worrying about finding a relationship with a man, I'm going to simply trust God and build my relationship with Him."

During this time, some of my friends made dreadful choices in second marriages, so it wasn't hard for me to adopt the philosophy, "Better no husband than a bad husband." However, Allison was at a stage of life when she really wanted someone to be a dad for her. She frequently gave me not-so-subtle suggestions like, "Mom, let's face it. No one is asking you out. Are you sure you're wearing enough makeup?"

Allison became my constant companion during this time. Even when I attended conferences, seminars, and training events, I took her with me whenever possible. I greatly enjoyed her company, and it helped insulate me from impulsively forming any new relationships.

But in the spring of 1997, I signed up for an Israel tour, which was scheduled for June. Even though I had sent in my payment, however, in May I had a real sense in my gut that I shouldn't go on the trip. Not really knowing why, I canceled the trip.

In the meantime, I received an invitation to attend a conference in Jacksonville, and this included an opportunity to meet with some intercessors who would be praying for the city. I passed the invitation on to my friend Gloria, thinking the conference might interest her, because I really had no interest in it at the time.

Much to my surprise, however, Gloria called me soon afterward and said, "The Lord told me to take you to that conference in Jacksonville. I'm going to pay your way, and this time you aren't supposed to take Allison with you."

I had known Gloria for many years, and she had always been right on target with the things she heard from the Lord. So I hardly even questioned her words, sensing in my heart that it was important for me to go without Allison.

Little did I know that Thursday, June 12, 1997, was my date with destiny—the day that would change everything. Remember the story in Joshua 3 about the Israelites crossing the Jordan River, leaving the wilderness behind them, and entering the Promised Land? That's the kind of transformation God did in my heart that day. After years of quiet desperation as a worn-out and wounded widow, I discovered a surprising life of *"inexpressible and glorious joy"* (1 Pet. 1:8 NIV).

I had been a counselor in need of healing from the Wonderful Counselor—Jesus Christ. But I wasn't the only one being prepared for a date with destiny that day. The Lord had been bringing Dennis through some difficult but amazing transformations of his own.

Chapter 3

A PASTOR AT THE END OF HIS ROPE

By Dennis

Beauty for Ashes

In the spring of 1997, I was at the end of my rope. After years as a successful Pennsylvania pastor—bringing hope and healing to others—my own life was now in shambles. Behind the scenes, I had struggled for years to salvage my troubled marriage. But the end finally came. My 25-year marriage ended in divorce, and I resigned as pastor of the church I had planted many years before. Needless to say, I was devastated. Losing both my marriage and my ministry brought overwhelming confusion and pain.

"What should I do now?" I wondered. "I feel called to ministry, but how can I serve God in ministry again? Even if the Lord forgives me and restores me, will people ever accept a divorced pastor as their leader?"

I felt like a failure, a washed-up leader, and a hopeless case for God to ever use again. I knew God hated divorce (see Mal. 2:16),

43

and the demons of hell were screaming their loudest that He hated me as well.

Yet in the midst of my pain, God spoke to me that He was bringing me into a year of jubilee and a time of restoration. Despite my failed marriage, He hadn't given up on me. And one day a man of God singled me out of a crowd and encouraged me with the words of Proverbs 24:16 (NASB): *"A righteous man falls seven times, and rises again."*

My situation stood in stark contrast with God's promises outlined in Isaiah 61. At a time when I saw bad news on every side, the Lord promised "good tidings" (v. 1); after my years of endeavoring to heal people's broken lives, now the Lord wanted to heal my own broken heart (v. 1); despite the trauma of losing my marriage and ministry, He wanted to give me liberty from captivity (v. 1); as I mourned and experienced the grief process, He promised to console me and give me comfort (vs. 2-3); though my entire life was desolate and in ruins, He said He would rebuild me into His image (v. 4); and through it all, He offered me the "great exchange": beauty for ashes, the oil of joy for mourning, and the garment of praise for the spirit of heaviness (v. 3).

Despite such wonderful promises for deep healing and restoration, I was painfully aware that my life was a mess. So when I heard or read promises like this, it was hard not to conclude that the Lord was just "messing with me." It was difficult to imagine life free from my current emotional baggage. It was hard to imagine life outside of my present circumstances.

I was a basket case, a candidate for a major overhaul. And even if God could eventually restore me, I was sure it would be five, ten, or fifteen years before I would be ready for ministry again. But God had other plans.

Promises Amid Problems

For years I'd been intrigued by the description of Abraham in Hebrews 11:8: *"By faith Abraham obeyed when he was called to go out to the place which he would receive as an inheritance. And he went out, not knowing where he was going."* It was bad enough that Abraham was called toward a destiny he didn't understand, but in order to obey God and receive his promised inheritance, he had to leave behind everything that was comfortable and familiar (see Gen. 12:1-2). The Lord said he would end up in *"a land that I will show you,"* but it would have been nice to know a little more detail beforehand. Of course, we know now that the story had a happy ending. God fulfilled His promise: *"I will bless you and make your name great; and you shall be a blessing"* (Gen. 12:2).

Like Abraham, I was sensing God leading me to leave my comfort zone in Pennsylvania and venture out to a new territory, both geographically and spiritually. But it was hard to be confident my story would have a happy ending. Yet at times I heard God promising to bless me and make me a blessing again in ministry to others. Though, truth be told, I couldn't see a straight path toward that outcome.

At one point, when I was still in full-time ministry, I distinctly heard God promise to meet all my financial needs without needing to seek secular employment again. With my ministry gone and only a few months of savings in my bank account, it was difficult to comprehend how the Lord would ever fulfill this now. Still hurt and confused, it wasn't easy to trust my inner sense of God's will. Yet somehow He enabled me to feel moments of hope that He truly could bring beauty out of my ashes.

Launching Out

Having no idea why, I was feeling an increasing desire to move to Charlotte, North Carolina. Giving me no details, the Lord impressed Jeremiah 29:7 on my heart as some sort of future assignment: *"Seek the peace of the city where I have caused you to be carried away captive, and pray to the Lord for it; for in its peace you will have peace."*

It would have been one thing if Charlotte was a place where I already had family or friends. A ready-made support system would have been nice at that point in my life. But it was neither of those. I knew no one in Charlotte, and I had no plans for what I was to do when I arrived there. No family. No friends. No job. No ministry. Charlotte was no more than a point on the map to me. Yet in March 1997, I packed up a few belongings in my car and left for an uncertain future, hundreds of miles away from my roots.

What a strange sensation it was. I felt like a man without a country. I had lived for years in familiar surroundings. I drove the same route to work each day, got my hair cut at the same place, and used the same dry cleaners. I had a great support system of friends in Pennsylvania. I knew all the other local pastors in my area, and several of them had been dear friends for many years. My life had practically been on autopilot.

While I enjoyed the stability and predictability of my Pennsylvania roots, I was aware that comfort zones can become coffins if we aren't willing to lay things down to follow God's call. I found myself in a position like the four lepers who asked themselves: *"Why do we sit here until we die?"* (2 Kings 7:3 NASB). Staying would mean eventual "death," while leaving in obedience to God would mean a new life.

But why Charlotte? I had never even visited this city I was planning to make my new home. I didn't know a soul there. And when friends asked for my new contact information, I couldn't even give them an address or phone number. I thought I may have been just going crazy. I felt confused and alone as I approached the city I hoped would be my place of new beginnings.

Strange Signposts

Something extraordinary happened as I crossed into the Charlotte city limits. In a flash, my mind's eye saw a city map suddenly burst into flames, just like the Ponderosa map in the opening sequence of the popular *Bonanza* television series years ago.

This experience was both exciting and bewildering. Although it seemed an encouraging confirmation that the Lord had something special in mind for me in Charlotte, it also reminded me I had absolutely no idea what the future would hold there.

I've never been very good at following maps and directions (some would say, yes, I'm a typical man). Not knowing my way around Charlotte, I drove straight through the city on I-77 and nearly ended up in South Carolina. Seeing Exit 1, I realized I needed to get off the freeway immediately or else I'd be past Charlotte.

"Lead me, Lord!" I whispered a nervous prayer of both hope and desperation. Without any particular destination in mind, I turned onto the exit ramp and just kept driving. I knew of several churches in the area and wanted to find my church home before proceeding with other decisions.

Somehow, I ended up on South Polk Street on the southern edge of Charlotte. When I noticed a small metal building with children's playground equipment and cars parked outside, I decided to stop and ask directions to a local church with which I was familiar.

As I pulled into the parking lot, I noticed a man sitting in one of the cars. I rolled down my window, but before I could even get a word out, the man said, "Are you going to ask for directions? The Lord told me to wait in the car, because someone was going to ask me for directions, and I needed to be here."

I was startled by the man's statement, but it was also tremendously encouraging. Immediately some of my feelings of aloneness left, and I was filled with reassurance that God was still very much with me. Although I felt completely lost in this strange new city, my heavenly Father had everything under control. Some sort of wonderful plan had been mapped out for me, and I was stumbling upon it with each new twist and turn of the road.

After the man gave me directions to a church I'd heard about in Charlotte, I found a nearby hotel where I could spend the night before embarking again on my new adventure the following day. That night I tossed and turned in anticipation of what the next day would hold.

Surprising Open Doors

The next day was Saturday, and I drove to the church the man had given me directions to. I didn't expect it to be open, but I wanted to make sure I could find it on Sunday morning. To my surprise, the building was open, and it turned out that an ushers' meeting was taking place. So I went inside and saw a bulletin board with notices of items for sale, students looking for Christian roommates, and apartments for rent.

I didn't have a lasting place to stay yet, and the hotel would be far too expensive for the long term. So I copied down a list of possibilities from the bulletin board, hoping to find a suitable Christian roommate and inexpensive rent.

I had purchased a cell phone before leaving Pennsylvania, but in those days cell phones servers charged exorbitant roaming and long-distance fees. Not wanting to use up minutes on my cell phone, I found a pay phone and began dialing the numbers for potential apartments. Much to my frustration, all the doors seemed to be closed. Some of the places had already been rented, and others were looking for a female roommate or a student in the ministry school. After one refusal after another, my list was pretty much exhausted.

I dialed one more number, and my heart sank as the woman on the other end of the line said, "No, I don't have anything." However, the power of God suddenly flooded the phone booth, and I was astonished to hear her say, "Oh, my! Oh, my! Can I call you back in a minute?"

Later, I discovered she had called a friend to pray, telling her, "Would you pray for me? I was talking to a man looking for a place to rent, and I told him a clear no. But then I heard the Lord say, 'Do something for this man!'"

After a few minutes, the woman called me back at the phone booth and said, "Can you meet me for lunch?" At lunch, she told me she had a condominium I could "rent" from her. God had told her to let me stay there rent-free for as long as I liked, if I was willing to sign a lease—for a dollar.

Her condo was fully furnished—including towels, bed sheets, silverware, dishes, pots and pans, and a washer and dryer. It even had a deck overlooking a beautiful lake. When I moved in a few days later, I sat on the deck and cried at the goodness of God, being simply overwhelmed.

My life still seemed a mess, but the Lord was clearly moving. Like the earth is described in Genesis 1:2, I sometimes felt "formless and empty," and often "darkness was over the surface" of my life. But in the midst of the chaos and confusion, "the Spirit of God was hovering," working powerfully yet sometimes invisibly on my behalf.

Despite these signs of hope, I still couldn't help but wonder where the path would lead me. Yes, I could see unmistakable signs that God was blessing me, but could He truly make me a blessing to others again? And even though I was grateful He was beginning to heal my inner pain, it still was unfathomable that He could use me to bring deep relief to others in their distress. Yet one day the dark clouds parted and a breakthrough came, suddenly changing everything.

A Rendezvous with Destiny

For my entire Christian life, I had always been involved in a church, and that was my intention in Charlotte as well. But as you might imagine, this wasn't very easy to do. In Pennsylvania, I had been a senior pastor, a leader, a minister, a counselor, and a teacher. But I was here in a new city, and no one knew me. I was a nobody—and a divorced nobody at that. No one knew I had been in ministry, nor was I in any hurry to let anyone know. I was feeling fragile in my calling and uncertain about what my future ministry, if I had any, would look like.

Whenever I pondered involvement in the church I was attending in Charlotte, my mind was flooded with troubling questions. Would the church leadership feel threatened when they found out I had been a pastor? And what would they think when they learned I had been divorced? Would they ever allow a divorced person to be involved in ministry in any capacity?

Instead of fretting about whether I would be accepted or not, I decided to set my heart on finding ways to serve. And recalling the Scripture God had given me about praying for the city, I figured the best place to start was volunteering for the intercessory prayer team. It seemed like the safest and most inconspicuous place of service I could find.

It turned out that many of the intercessors were planning to go to Jacksonville, Florida, to pray for a big conference there. Without any source of income, my meager savings was diminishing daily, so I was pretty squeamish about making a trip to Florida. It seemed to make little sense to my natural mind, yet somehow I felt I was supposed to go.

Meanwhile, the pastor took me up on my offer to help out in any area where help was needed. He asked me to join eight other people in preparing 3,000 information packets for the upcoming conference. It was a big project, expected to take us the better part of a day.

While we were preparing the packets, one person suggested it would help pass the time if we went around the room and shared our testimonies. I inwardly groaned, feeling much too raw from recent events to want to share with a group of strangers. But I figured I just had to make the best of it.

It caught my attention when a young man shared that he was planning a cruise a few years prior, and God told him he would meet his wife on the cruise: "You will know she is the one," the Lord supposedly said to him, "because she will pray for you and then ask you to pray for her."

I thought this was a hilarious story. After all, believers pray for one another all the time, so how could that possibly stand out as unusual and mean that she was going to be his spouse? As I smugly chuckled to myself, the power of God hit me so hard that my knees almost buckled. To my amazement, the Lord distinctly said, "The same thing is going to happen to you, Dennis!"

"Wait a minute here," I silently protested. "Lord, this is much too soon to contemplate remarriage." Despite my initial misgivings, though, I recognized God's unmistakable voice. After wrestling with this for a while, I finally resolved in my heart: "Okay, Lord, maybe I would be open to consider marriage again five or ten years down the road. But certainly no sooner." Even with this faint openness to remarriage, I added one final requirement: "Father, there's no way I want to get married again unless my wife is my best friend." I had seen enough troubled marriages over the years to know that couples rarely survived the difficulties of life unless they had first become best friends.

Just a few days later, I drove down to Jacksonville to attend the conference. Little did I know that God was orchestrating a rendezvous with destiny. Expecting just to intercede and serve quietly behind the scenes, I was stunned when Thursday, June 12, 1997, became—as Jen has already described it—the day that changed everything.

OUR STORIES INTERSECT: MAKING ALL THINGS NEW

By Dr. Jen

The Sound of a Voice

Early on the morning of June 12, I waited on the side porch of my house in Waycross, Georgia, as my friend Gloria pulled into the driveway. We were taking an unfamiliar route north of Jacksonville, and Gloria was uncertain about the driving time to our destination. So we loaded the car as quickly as we could and sped off for our destination near the beach on the east side of Jacksonville.

Gloria and I arrived barely in time for the first session in the sanctuary, and it was too late to go looking for the intercessors' meeting room. As soon as the meeting concluded, though, we found someone with a staff badge on who led us to the room the intercessors were gathered in.

About 90 intercessors were meeting in a large room near the fellowship hall. During the afternoon meeting, the leaders asked for 15 volunteers to stay in a back room and pray throughout the conference, which would cause them to miss the main meetings. Even though I wanted to hear the speakers, Gloria immediately volunteered both of us for the back room. So when we came back to the church that evening after dinner, we went straight to the prayer room.

She Sounds Like Me

Someone suggested we pray for one another before interceding for the conference and the city of Jacksonville. Dennis later said that as people were praying for each other's personal needs, he overheard me praying for one of the other intercessors there. Once again, he was struck by a sudden surge of the power of God and his knees almost buckled. Before even turning to see who was praying, he thought, "She sounds like me when she prays." Then right after he wondered, "Hmmm...what does it even mean that 'she sounds like me'?" At that, Dennis looked to see whom he had heard. He turned toward me and our eyes met.

We spoke briefly, and I felt impressed to pray for him, so I asked if that was all right. After I prayed a little while, he acted like he was going to walk away, so I exclaimed, "Wait. I haven't finished praying yet!"

Dennis later explained that he was completely overwhelmed with everything going on. And he couldn't help but remember the story he heard a few days earlier of the couple who met on a cruise. The young man sharing the testimony had quoted the Lord as saying, "She will pray for you and then ask you to pray for her." But since the second part of the sentence didn't happen that night, Dennis tried to pass off the whole incident as just a coincidence.

During that whole evening, I kept hearing Dennis's voice as he prayed. I didn't particularly notice anything else about him, but his voice echoed in my ears and touched my heart. Sometimes the unguarded sound of a person's voice reveals their heart and core identity, and that's what I felt about Dennis as the intercessors prayed that night.

Although one might think matters of love and attraction are strange subjects for scientific study, they're actually hot topics for research right now. A scientist studying the science of romance was told in an interview: "I knew, when I first heard that voice, that he was for me." The scientist concluded that "the music of the voice [was] perhaps a better indication of a man's soul [than physical appearance]."[1]

When I read this scientist's observation, my thoughts instantly went back to the weekend when Dennis and I first met. As he prayed, the sound of his voice somehow resonated deep within my heart just as, Dennis said, my voice did with him.

Can We Be Friends?

The next morning we all went into the sanctuary, where the first two rows had been reserved for the intercessors. Gloria came in early and found a seat, but it turned out that there were two more intercessors than there were reserved seats. Since Dennis and I were the last to arrive, there were no reserved seats left. Instead, we found two seats together near the back of the room and had an opportunity to talk a bit.

When the session was over, Dennis asked if I would like to go somewhere for lunch. My thoughts raced. I hadn't been out with any man for almost five years, and I was in no hurry to change that at the time. I had told the Lord I was going to run from men, but I gave Him permission to stop me if He ever wanted to bring me another husband.

Rather than completely accept Dennis's invitation, I said I hadn't been out with anyone since my husband's death, but I would find my friend Gloria and the three of us could go together as a group. We drove to a nearby Quincy's Buffet, and when we found a table several other people from the conference asked if they could join us.

Ever since the evening before, I had been thinking, "I should have asked Dennis to pray for me." So I leaned toward him at our table and said, "When we get back to the church this afternoon, I want you to pray for me." I wasn't prepared for his reaction. First, Dennis's face turned white. Then he pushed his chair back from the table, turned to the side, and doubled over. I was so perplexed that I kept asking him, "What's wrong? What did I say?"

At first he didn't want to tell me, but I wouldn't let his over-reaction go without some kind of explanation. He later divulged that my probing caused him to pray in silent desperation, "Help, Lord! What am I supposed to say now?" The second part of the young couple's testimony—"and then she will ask you to pray for her"—was happening just like the Lord had spoken to Dennis only a few days before. Dennis later said, "I was completely over-whelmed with astonishment that Jen was my wife-to-be!"

Dennis remembered how he had qualified the thought of remarriage as being the union of best friends. So he told me the story of the couple and their testimony of praying for each other on the cruise. But he watered down the story's application to us, saying the Lord said He would send him a friend. Well, that melted my heart. "Of course I'll be your friend!" I assured him.

My First How-To

Later that afternoon, we discovered that the prayer room was locked, so Dennis, Gloria, and I sat on the carpet while the cleaning staff vacuumed around us. That's when Dennis prayed for me for the very first time.

As we closed our eyes, I learned my first how-to lesson from Dennis. He told me to open my heart, which confused me at first. Thinking of the physical heart, it took me a while to get his point. But when he gave me a little more instruction, I began to understand what he was referring to. He told me to put my hand on my belly and yield to Christ in my heart. He quoted the words of Jesus: *"He that believeth on Me, as the scripture hath said, out of his belly shall flow rivers of living water"* (John 7:38 KJV).

I had always thought my spiritual heart was where my physical heart was located, even though the Bible clearly said it was in the *belly*. Never before had I heard anyone tell someone else to yield his or her heart, where to yield, or even how to yield. But as I attempted to cooperate with what Dennis was telling me, he continually encouraged me, saying, "There, you're doing it."

At the same time, I could feel the difference inside my heart. I don't remember exactly what we prayed about, but looking back I can see that he led me through some how-tos for healing of the heart. I still didn't catch the full significance of what I was learning at the time. However, it was obvious that Dennis had a unique anointing and spiritual authority, and he was teaching principles that were entirely new to me.

Stepping into Destiny

By mid-afternoon, the intercessors had started trickling back to the church, and someone unlocked the prayer room. Since it wasn't yet time for the meeting to begin, people milled around and talked up and down the hall and in the room itself. I was standing in the hall talking to an intercessor I had just met, but Dennis was in the prayer room talking to someone else.

The first day of the conference, Dennis had seen someone he knew in the audience, and they caught each other's eye. They had not seen each other since then, so she came looking for him in the prayer room to say hello. Without any warning, she burst into the room, came over to Dennis, and exclaimed, "Have you met anyone?" That shook him, so he tried to make a joke and change the subject.

But she stopped him mid-sentence. "No, wait!" she demanded. "I'm speaking to you as an intercessor, not as a friend. Come out here into the hall." At that, she grabbed Dennis's arm and pulled him to the door. Then she pointed down the hall at me. "When I was walking down the hall, I could see you...married to *her*!"

At the very same time, the intercessor I was talking to reached out and clasped my hands. Drawing an imaginary line on the floor with her foot, she pulled me across the line and said, "The Lord is saying to you, 'Step into your destiny, Jen!'"

By now Dennis was on emotional overload. Significant praying was impossible. So he walked over to the sanctuary door and peered at the musicians on the stage. The usher standing near the door looked at him and queried, "Are you looking for your wife... the one with the white top and blue print skirt?" He described my outfit exactly. Unable to respond coherently, Dennis inhaled deeply and closed the door. This was just too much to take in at one time.

The Big Meltdown

Remember the story I told in the second chapter about the emotional meltdown of a young woman named Amanda? This happened the following afternoon, when the intercessors were praying for those in Jacksonville who were held captive to fear or intimidation.

Suddenly, Amanda collapsed to the floor. Dennis went over to pray with her, while the rest of us were stunned into inaction. Yet I was close enough to see what was taking place and hear how Dennis was praying for her.

He guided her in praying through multiple areas of fears and hurts. One at a time, he addressed each new area that came up. Only after she felt true relief did Dennis move on to another issue. Remarkably, it took only a few minutes to address each area of fear, but Amanda could tell she was experiencing real inner transformation.

All the intercessors were gathered around, watching with amazement. I was blown away by how much emotional pain was dealt with and how fast the relief came to her. I had seen lots of counseling and psychological therapy over the years, but nothing like this.

"Wow!" I thought. "This is the answer everyone is yearning for!" I felt like I had just witnessed something as monumental as the cure for "emotional cancer." It was the missing ingredient needed to heal wounded people and a troubled church. Here, at last, was the secret for healing emotional pain quickly and efficiently. Stunned by this rapid, visible transformation, the person in charge of the meeting stood with her mouth wide open and incredulously asked the pastor, "Who are you?"

From Prayer Partners to Life Partners

After Dennis intervened to bring Amanda quick relief during her emotional meltdown, things also moved forward very quickly in our relationship. By the time the evening came and the sun had set, we were together every possible moment.

Only days earlier, we had just been strangers volunteering to pray at a conference. Along the way, God led us to pray for each other, which was a significant step. However, in record time the Lord took us from being strangers to being prayer partners to an amazing peace and excitement that He might be bonding us together as partners for life. My friend Gloria said later that she was starting to feel like a chaperone for madly-in-love high school kids.

As the days unfolded, it became clear that this was the first step in God fulfilling His promise to make *"all things new"* in both of our lives (Rev. 21:5). I call it the day that changed everything, because that's exactly what the Lord did—He changed *everything* for me and for Dennis. Seeing a counselor who needed healing and a pastor at the end of his rope, He looked down with His incredible mercy to bring us hope and healing.

The conference was over Saturday night, so Sunday morning Dennis drove back to Charlotte and I returned home to Waycross. But Dennis called me that evening and we talked for five hours. As I sat talking with him, Allison sat down at the kitchen table and watched in amazement. This was quite a strange event she was witnessing. Her mom was actually talking with a man.

Dennis called again the following night, and this time he decided to tell me the whole story about the young couple who met on the cruise, prayed for each other, and were married a short time later. This time he admitted that the Lord had used the word *wife*.

The phone calls were wonderful, but the tension of not seeing each other was becoming too much to bear. Waycross was a six-hour drive from Charlotte, but Dennis left early the next day and arrived at my house by noon.

Gloria and her husband invited Dennis to stay with them while he was in town, and he ended up staying for a whole week. We talked nonstop, and I was thrilled to get to know him. We had the same heart in so many areas, and we already were openly talking about marriage. At the end of the week, Dennis had to return to Charlotte, but Allison and I made plans to drive there for the Fourth of July.

Although we wanted to get married as soon as possible, I knew I would need to work at first. So I began checking on job openings in Charlotte. Even before Allison and I visited the area, I had three interviews lined up. So Allison and I reserved a room at the Days Inn. In addition to having a great time seeing the area, I was thrilled by how well Allison hit it off with Dennis. One highlight was when he took her roller skating, skated with her, and taught her how to skate backward.

New Job, New Home, New Life

By the end of the week in Charlotte, I had three job offers. So now the three of us went house hunting together. I had a large old house in Waycross, with a lot of furniture, so we checked out real estate with my furniture in mind. For several days, we didn't see anything that would even remotely work. The houses were too dark, too small, too poorly designed, or too far from town. There was always something prohibiting us from choosing it.

So the three of us drove to look around in nearby Rock Hill, South Carolina, and we pulled into a fast-food parking lot to pray. "Lord, please help!" Time was running out, and Allison and I would be returning to Waycross soon.

We pulled out of the parking lot, drove a few blocks, and then felt led to pull into a neighborhood near Winthrop University. It was an older section of town, and huge oak trees formed a canopy over the roads. We made another turn, and there was a grey ranch-style house with a For Sale by Owner sign in front. So we parked on the street, got out, and rang the doorbell. An attractive woman answered the door but asked us to give her about 30 minutes to straighten up the house before giving us a tour. We ate a bite of lunch, then drove back and rang the doorbell once again.

The exterior of the house was simple, but the interior was quite charming. It had a large living room and dining room, as well as a knotty pine-paneled study with built-in bookshelves. The breakfast nook had a lovely stained glass window. A very large master suite had been added at the rear, and there was another stained glass window in the master bathroom.

I was walking with the owner, Janice, as she pointed out the various features, but Allison and Dennis were walking behind us. She was holding onto Dennis's arm and whispering into his ear, repeatedly saying, "This is it. This is the one! Do you think Mom knows that this is it? Should we tell her?"

Janice was a schoolteacher and was hoping to sell her house and move into a new home by the time the new school year started. She let me sign a contract contingent on my house selling, and agreed to hold it for two weeks.

Allison and I said good-bye to Dennis and we drove back to Waycross. I spread the word that my house was for sale and had a buyer in just two days—with cash. I was so happy I could call Janice and finalize the purchase of our new home in Rock Hill.

Plans and Purpose

God has wonderful plans for each of our lives (see Jer. 29:11), and it was great to see all the pieces coming together for my new job and our new home. The next step was to plan our wedding and moving arrangements. Even with details like these, we sensed

God's favor and guidance. As Proverbs 16:9 (NLT) says, *"We can make our plans, but the Lord determines our steps."* Dennis and I were married informally August 6, 1997, but then we had a formal wedding ceremony on August 30.

As Allison and I prepared to leave Waycross behind, Dennis was concerned about how she would feel about leaving her school and friends. But as she buckled her seatbelt to depart for her new life in Charlotte, she turned to Dennis and said, "Thank goodness you are taking us out of this one-horse town!" I had always thought Waycross was a charming small town, perfect for raising children, but Allison was clearly looking forward to city life.

When we arrived back in Charlotte, I was delighted to meet Dennis's landlady, who had generously let him stay in her condo for one dollar. She said when she saw us, "Listen, you two, God didn't bring you together just for your own pleasure. He brought you together for a kingdom purpose."

Her word of encouragement was so true. And to think it all started with two broken people who were first intercessors and prayer partners. God used "the sound of a voice" to bring us together to obey His voice and reflect His glory.

ENDNOTE

1.   N. Doidge, *The Brain that Changes Itself* (New York: Penguin Group, Inc., 2007), 101.

Part Two

THE POWER OF
SIMPLE PRAYER

Interlude

THE PURPOSE OF SIMPLE PRAYER

By Dennis

I want to introduce simple prayer, which is really daily prayer and learning to abide in Christ, that sprang out of my own prayer life, developed over a period of 30-something years. It is a beginning step into making sure our intimacy with God grows, and our abiding in Him is real and relational. There are a few preliminaries I would like to clear up before jumping into this section. I want to introduce three major phrases that are vital for simple prayer: how to connect, how to stay connected, and the need to reconnect when we break our abiding life.

Ultimately, we're called to live an abiding lifestyle, walking in the presence of God on a continual basis. And we are to train ourselves to constantly get better and better at it every day. Yes, we're all in school, we're all in a process of learning how to abide. But Jen and I desire to place in your hands some tools to help you increase your intimacy with God and to strengthen your relationship with Him.

To Connect

To connect with God is a very essential ingredient in our pursuit of simple prayer. If we're believers, then Christ resides within us and we have Him dwelling in our hearts. But even though this is true for us, we must still learn to abide, which means it is a process that we will get better at over time.

Proverbs 3:5-6 tells us, *"Trust in the Lord with all your heart, and lean not on your own understanding; in all your ways acknowledge Him, and He shall direct your paths."* When Proverbs tells us to *"acknowledge Him,"* it means we are to acknowledge Christ dwelling within us, recognizing the divine intimate contact we have with Him. To connect with Him, then, means that we're cultivating a connection with Him and an awareness of His presence within us. The more we do this, the more fully and completely we learn to abide in Him.

Our awareness of His presence increases with practice, with time spent in prayer, and by acknowledging the personhood of God dwelling within us. Acknowledging Him is one of the goals of simple prayer. We are not just acknowledging Him as residing in heaven (which seems to put Him far away), or simply acknowledging Him with our mind (though we do this sometimes), but we are acknowledging Christ within us (which is the hope of glory). As we develop that intimate contact with Him on a regular basis, then the promise is that He will direct our paths, which is ultimately what we want Him to do. We should all desire Him to be in charge of our life, for Him to live His life through us rather than us living our life for Him.

This connection begins in our prayer time in the morning, but staying connected is a lifelong learning process.

Stay Connected

John says, *"But if we walk in the light as He is in the light, we have fellowship with one another, and the blood of Jesus Christ His Son cleanses us from all sin"* (1 John 1:7). When we're cleansed from all sin and walking in the light, having fellowship with both Christ and one another, then we're basically walking in the peace of God, clean and connected with Him. The way we can continually stay connected to Him is through allowing His blood to cleanse us from all sin—at any moment and in any place—allowing us to walk in the light with Him.

Jesus said, *"Abide in Me, and I in you. As the branch cannot bear fruit of itself, unless it abides in the vine, neither can you, unless you abide in Me"* (John 15:4). So we not only want to connect with Him during our prayer time each morning, but it's essential that we stay connected throughout our daily lives. The beautiful thing of staying connected with Christ is that it isn't dependent on our circumstances. We can enjoy an intimate communion with Him at all times and in any situation.

When it comes to simple prayer, the challenge is in learning to abide in Him throughout every moment of every day. Getting connected to Him is easy, but staying connected takes a bit more practice. It is simple, but it is also foundational and essential in our walk with God. We must come to the place of learning to abide in Him so that we can more effectively remain connected to Him.

Staying connected to Him is going to be a challenge for any believer. Therefore, there will be times where we break connection with Him. But, fortunately for us, there is a provision for reconnecting.

To Reconnect

Many of us have been surprised by impulses, thoughts, and emotions that seem to come out of the blue and throw us off course. And oftentimes, we enter into sinful behavior and yield to the temptation. So there is a need to promptly reconnect with Christ in an intimate and life-giving way. It doesn't have to be long, drawn-out process, but it does have to be prompt and intentional.

The Bible promises that if we confess our sins, He is faithful to forgive us our sins and to cleanse us from all unrighteousness (see 1 John 1:9). John isn't speaking of a process of repentance and penance that we perform to get in God's good graces, but an instantaneous cleansing of unrighteousness, resulting in a restoration of our connection with Christ. We can once again begin to walk in fellowship with Him and with one another.

When we break fellowship with Him, however, we have an Advocate with the Father through Jesus Christ:

> *My little children, these things I write to you, so that you may not sin. And if anyone sins, we have an Advocate with the Father, Jesus Christ the righteous. And He Himself is the propitiation for our sins, and not for ours only but also for the whole world* (1 John 2:1-2).

The provision for being reconnected with God quickly and effectively is the atoning sacrifice of Jesus Christ on our behalf. Because of His shed blood, we can walk in an abiding lifestyle with the Father, sensing His peace and feeling His presence throughout every moment of every day.

Three Ingredients

These are the three essential ingredients to understand if simple prayer is going to help us cultivate the ability to connect with Christ within, to stay connected to Him, and also to reconnect when we break our fellowship with Him.

Since apart from Him we can do nothing, our goal through simple prayer is to make our connection with Christ both stronger and thicker. Just like a branch connected to a tree trunk, the thicker the branch, the stronger the connection will be, and the greater its ability to bear fruit. The fruit of abiding is that we would all be His disciples, and that we would all bear much fruit (both good works as well as the fruit of the Spirit flowing from our lives). And that is what brings glory to the Father.

Chapter 5

CONNECTING IN THE SPIRITUAL REALM

By Dennis

Stunted Spiritual Growth

In the previous chapters of this book, Dr. Jen and I shared some of our own stories, then how our stories intersected and made all things new. Both of us have experienced what it's like to be broken people in need of deep relief through God's healing touch. Although we both were believers before the Lord showed us the principles of DRN (deep relief now), our spiritual growth was stunted by inner turmoil and emotional pain.

Sharing our story was just a prelude to what this book is really about, which is showing you how to experience deep relief in your own life. As the book unfolds, we'll also be sharing some brief stories of how God has already used DRN to quickly transform countless others.

Lord of Our Life

God wants to be the Lord of our entire life, not just our "spiritual" life. Since He made us as thinking, willing, and feeling beings, He wants us to let Him be Lord of our thoughts, choices, and emotions. Though we often make a dichotomy between our "natural" life and our "spiritual" life, God makes no such distinction. Rather, He cares about us as individuals, as whole people who have a spirit, a soul, and a body.

Throughout the Scriptures we're told that God's thoughts are higher than our thoughts (see Isa. 55:8-9; Rom. 11:33-34), His will is superior to the choices we would make on our own (see Prov. 14:12; 3:5-7), and His love is superior to our carnal emotions (see 1 Cor. 13; 1 John 2:15-17). But though He is above and beyond us, He still wants to relate to us in true intimacy. He is not a God who cannot be known, but rather a Person desiring to reveal Himself to us on a continual basis.

But in order to connect with Him in a real way, we have to understand the connection between the flesh and the spirit. Even though God made us as thinking, feeling, and willing beings, He wants all three of those areas to be ruled by the Spirit of God; that we would be described as people who "walk in the Spirit" or are "Spirit led."

The word *spirit* or *spirits* is used more than 900 times throughout the Scriptures. Jesus told us that God is Spirit, but He also told us that God is known and worshiped through the human spirit: *"God is Spirit, and those who worship Him must worship in spirit and truth"* (John 4:24). This means that a spiritual God communicates with man in the spiritual realm.

Since God has created us to be spiritual people, He has called us to connect with Him on a spiritual level. But sometimes we have thoughts and emotions that are clearly not godly, and we often make choices that don't reflect His will for us. Our relationship with Him isn't about us having all the right answers, but about us connecting with Him on a spiritual level.

Supernatural Is Too Quiet

After Elijah was responsible for killing the prophets of Baal, he suddenly began to run for his life from the evil Jezebel. After going a day's journey into the wilderness, he came to a tree and sat under it. He was totally dejected and discouraged. But after an angel came and fed him, God spoke to him and told him to go to the top of the mountain. And here is what happened when he got there:

> *And behold, the Lord passed by, and a great and strong wind tore into the mountains and broke the rocks in pieces before the Lord, but the Lord was not in the wind; and after the wind an earthquake, but the Lord was not in the earthquake; and after the earthquake a fire, but the Lord was not in the fire; and after the fire a still small voice* (1 Kings 19:11-12).

Even though there were major occurrences that took place—hurricane, fire, and an earthquake—the Bible says that God wasn't in any of those. Rather, we are told that there was a "still small voice" the Lord was present in. One translation calls it a "delicate whisper."

The point I want to make here is that most supernatural occurrences are too quiet for our flesh. There's a supernatural that can arrest our attention—a miracle of physical healing for example. These are instantaneous things that defy the laws of nature, being completely evident that God has broken into our realm. But the truth is that those things are not normal—they are not constant. In a lifetime we may have seen many miracles, but we don't see them every single day. The biggest miracle, of course, is salvation, and salvation is a total transformation of an individual's life. And yet the miracle of an ongoing relationship is learning that the supernatural realm in which we live is basically too quiet for our flesh.

So if we're going to discuss the connection between flesh and spirit, the first thing we need to resolve in our heart is that we're going to have to endeavor to quiet our flesh to really connect with God in the spiritual realm. We will not learn spiritual things when our mind is loud, when our actions are boisterous, and when we're emotionally restless. All of that clatter will prevent us from making a proper kind of connection with our spirits. Our thoughts, our emotions, and our flesh need to be quieted in order to hear God and connect with Him on a deeper level.

In order to connect with God and experience His thoughts, His love, and His will, we're going to have to move beyond being biblically literate and realize that the two wings of the dove are Word and Spirit. The Word we can learn with our mind, but God ultimately wants the reality of that Word in our hearts. That means it's going to take spiritual insight and spiritual impact for those two to come together.

It's actually this lack of connection between flesh and spirit that has caused such slow growth in the Christian life for many of us. We know our Bible backward and forward, but there is very little application or sensitivity to the Spirit of God because of the connection problem between our heads and our spirits. We need to know how to connect with God, not theoretically, but experientially and subjectively. We have to know the difference between flesh and spirit.

God wants us to connect with Him on a spiritual level. He's not going to compromise and tell us that because we're noisy and loud in our heart that He's going to shout at us in order to get our attention. The delicate whisper to Elijah is the perfect example. God's often not in the wind, He's not in the fire, and He's not in the earthquake. We need recognize the delicate whisper when He shows up.

Practical Example

When I was a young Christian, one of the most beautiful experiences I had was when I was sleeping. Now, you have to understand that I am a heavy sleeper. The wind, fire, and earthquake Elijah experienced would have had a hard time waking me up. But I remember waking up in the middle of the night, and it felt like someone took a feather and brushed it on my spirit. It was a wooing from God to get up and pray. My body was dead tired and my flesh wanted to sleep. But I yielded to that gentle whisper. It could have been so easy to dismiss, but I knew that I knew it was God.

Do you want to know how I got out of bed? I simply put one leg out of bed and let gravity do the rest. I kind of rolled out of bed, got on the side of it, and began to pray. I don't even know how awake I really was, but I had the experience of a lifetime because God so established in my heart that that was exactly the experience He wanted for me at that moment in time.

We tend to notice earthquakes because they're loud and clear; it's evident even to the natural senses that something is going on. But most supernatural is too quiet for our flesh. How many spiritual experiences have we missed because we're too noisy (in our flesh)? How many times has God shown up, and we missed Him because we were looking for the spectacular (fire, earthquakes, and winds) but He was in the gentle whisper?

When we go to pray, our mind is plagued with thoughts. We think we need more coffee, or we need to throw another load of laundry in the wash, or we need to open our Bible. Or maybe we need to go check the door to see if the dog came back yet. Or perhaps we should check the garage for a couple of quarts of oil that we may need to pick up at AutoZone later in the day. If it's not one of those excuses, I'm sure you are thinking of many of your own that go through your head as you sit down to pray. But there's always something. All that means is that we haven't met Him yet; we are still at the mercy of our flesh.

Flesh or Spirit

The flesh is not like God's nature at all. Either flesh rules or the spirit rules at any given time. Paul said, *"For the flesh lusts against the Spirit, and the Spirit against the flesh; and these are contrary to one another, so that you do not do the things that you wish"* (Gal. 5:17). This is the real goal for spirit-to-Spirit contact with God.

There's a battle taking place between our spirit and our flesh. Who determines the victor in this battle? Who determines whether our flesh or our spirit is going to win? We do. Knowing that the battle is flesh against spirit, and knowing that God is going to meet us spirit to Spirit if we want to connect with Him, He's not going to meet with us on our standard, but He wants us to submit to His standard. Our standard normally consists of asking God to quickly speak to us, and speak loudly, because we have to go to work soon. But that is a sure way to get frustrated. Or we think because we put in our 20 minutes in the morning, that now it's time to go because we punched our spiritual timecard.

But the only thing that proves is that we never got in the spirit; we never met with Him spirit to Spirit. When we wean, quiet, and still the flesh and get into His presence, when it's time to go to work and we withdraw from that prayer closet, we're going to feel like something is being torn right out of our hearts. We won't want to leave if we're truly connecting with God on a spiritual level. If we don't have that on a regular basis, then we're not praying.

Eventually God will teach us that we don't have to leave Him. There's a special intimacy in that prayer closet, that what we touched in there we carry with us like precious cargo the rest of the day. He quickens a spiritual awareness where we practice the presence of God, which is a progressive learning curve. But it will never progress unless we try, unless we quiet our flesh and stop doing busy stuff, including religious activities that do not include the Holy Spirit, erroneously calling it devotions.

Spirit to Spirit

Devotions are not a head-to-head connection with God. Real devotion happens spirit to Spirit. We connect with God spirit to Spirit by quieting the flesh, the soul, and yielding to the Spirit of God within us. This is what happens when we pray—or maybe I should say this is what *should* happen when we pray. To walk in the Spirit, we must learn to maintain a spiritual connection with God in our everyday life.

David knew this well. He prayed, *"Surely I have calmed and quieted my soul, like a weaned child with his mother; like a weaned child is my soul within me"* (Ps. 131:2). Until we've had that experience ourselves, we haven't prayed. And the more often we commit to a spirit-to-Spirit relationship, the better we get at it. Our relationship with Him is magnetic, which means it gets easier the longer we spend with Him. So there's no reason to get discouraged, because relationships only grow stronger when they're done properly.

Spiritual Discernment

If we live by the [Holy] Spirit, let us also walk by the Spirit. [If by the Holy Spirit we have our life in God, let us go forward walking in line, our conduct controlled by the Spirit] (Galatians 5:25 AMP).

There's something I heard many years ago and has never left me since to show how important it is that we walk in a spirit-to-Spirit relationship with God: You can fool people with your words, you can fool people with your gestures, but you can't hide what emanates from you. What emanates from us is determined by our relationship with God.

Of course, we can either emanate good or bad—Jesus said, *"For out of the abundance of the heart the mouth speaks"* (Luke 6:45). Whatever is overflowing in our heart is going to come out of our mouth, but also out of our entire persona. If it's mostly flesh, we'll emanate flesh; but if it's mostly God, we'll emanate God. But one thing is certain: out of the overflow of our heart we will emanate. We cannot hide what emanates from us.

Real spiritual discernment knows what's going on in the spiritual realm. Body language is a physical observation; it's external—it's the way man judges things. Man judges by the outward appearance, but God judges by the heart.

Since we're spiritual people, we're supposed to discern all things. The spiritual man differentiates all things: *"But he that is spiritual, discerneth all things: yet he himself is judged of no man."* (1 Cor. 2:15 GNV). Everyone in the church is a spiritual person. If we're truly spiritual people, then we should be living by making spiritual distinctions. And by spiritual distinctions, I mean that the discerning of spirits is the ability to discern the spirit world: evil spirits, human spirits, and the Holy Spirit.

Real discernment sees more Holy Spirit than evil spirits. God is the only One who is omnipresent. We cannot be fooled by someone who has all this discernment for demons but they couldn't recognize the Holy Spirit if He was wearing a red baseball cap, as a well-known Christian preacher once commented. The real test of discernment is knowing God, knowing His nature, and being so acclimated to His nature that counterfeits stick out like a sore thumb.

A definition of the discerning of spirits from a note in my Bible says: "Discerning of spirits is the ability to discern the spirit world, and especially to detect the source of circumstances or motives of people."[1] The motives of people can be described as what is flavoring their spirits. We can often hear someone say something, but sometimes the flavor attached to their words is being motivated by something other than the love of God.

I've gone to the mall where someone standing at a kiosk in the center wants to sell you something. They want to rub cream on my hands (usually Jennifer's hands, not mine), and she'll say no. And they'll say, "Thank you, have a nice day." But what's coming from their heart is, "Go jump off a bridge." That's what it feels like in the spiritual realm. Why? Because we didn't cooperate with them and we didn't buy anything from them, but they are trying to be polite. So their words are saying one thing but their heart is somewhere else. The same is possible for a believer.

Discernment makes a distinction between flesh and spirit; it makes a distinction between the Holy Spirit, the human spirit, and evil spirits. It differentiates between those three areas. Every one of us has that capacity residing within us. But if we don't have a prayer life where we quiet our flesh and meet Him spirit to Spirit, we'll never learn the legitimate nature of Christ well enough to differentiate with all the counterfeits, all the flavors, and all of the nuances.

It is important for us to learn discernment and what it means to live in the spiritual realm. We have to have a prayer life if we are truly going to learn discernment and connect with God on a spirit-to-Spirit level. The key ingredient in that prayer life is in connecting with God. We cannot just look at our clock and see how much time we've spent with Him. We have to quiet our flesh and make a spirit-to-Spirit connection. But in order to do that, we need to know the location of our heart.

ENDNOTE

1. *Spirit-Filled Life Bible* (New King James Version), ed. Jack Hayford, (Nashville, TN: Thomas Nelson Publishers, 1991), 1737. This definition was taken from the note on 1 Corinthians 12:10.

Chapter 6

LOCATION, LOCATION, LOCATION

By Dennis

A Good Question

Many of us who are already Christians may be asking ourselves at this point, "Why haven't I already been healed of my emotional pain? I pray, read my Bible, and attend church—yet my emotional baggage never seems to go away."

That's a great question, and I can assure you that you're not alone in asking it. Some people don't even realize that God is able to give them deep relief from their inner pain. Others have adopted the misguided notion that the Lord is not willing to heal them—choosing to let them struggle throughout life with psychological hang-ups as some sort of "cross to bear." However, in many cases, we believe God's healing touch is possible, but we simply don't know how to access it.

When I first met Jen, I could tell right away that she was very intelligent and well educated. She was an intellectual, used to living her life in the cognitive realm—in her head rather than her heart. Because Jen approached life primarily through mental analysis, she struggled to understand what was happening when she prayed or worshiped. Most of her prayer life was a matter of prayer lists and petitions, but this didn't result in true intimacy with the Lord.

Through her analytical approach, she was able to learn many facts *about* God, but her mind-set wasn't very conducive to a close relationship *with* Him. The relational aspect of her spiritual life was more accidental than purposeful. Although she avidly read books about the prayer lives of great men and women of God, she was starving for more of God's reality in her own life.

The first thing I taught Jen was what had happened when she asked Jesus into her heart, and how to continue to encounter Jesus through prayer. I think you will be greatly helped by this vital first lesson of deep relief now.

What Prayer Really Entails

Some people treat prayer much the same as little children who send their gift requests to Santa Claus at Christmas. Without seeking any relationship, they expectantly mail their letters to Santa at the North Pole. But prayer is meant to be much more than this. In prayer we give the Lord access to our innermost being—our heart—so He heals us, transforms us, and gives us revelation and guidance.

There are deep places in the human heart that we all tend to hide and cover up through fear and denial. But God uses His Word and His Spirit to shine the light of healing on the dark and hidden places of our heart. The only thing a minister should do is facilitate what the Holy Spirit is already doing in the hearts and lives of individuals. The writer of Proverbs reminds us: *"Counsel in the heart of man is like water in a deep well, but a man of understanding draws it out"* (20:5 AMP).

After Jen and I got married, she asked me to disciple her in prayer. She was still working as a psychologist for that first year until she joined me in full-time ministry, but after she got home we ate dinner and spent time praying together. Out of these prayer times, we developed the how-tos we now teach to others wherever we go.

Have you ever thought about how significant it was that the disciples asked Jesus, *"Lord, teach us to pray"* (Luke 11:1)? There's no record of them ever asking Him the how-tos of healing the sick, casting out demons, or teaching the Word of God, but they wanted to know how to pray. Why? Because they saw this was the key to everything else Jesus did in His life and ministry.

The Location of the Heart

Many believers are confused about the difference between their head and their heart. They wonder if prayer is simply a matter of having the right thoughts in their head, or whether there should also be some other component—a matter of the heart and emotions—engaged as well.

During the eighteenth century, a French philosopher named Blaise Pascal once wrote, "There is a God-shaped hole in the heart of every man which cannot be filled by any created thing, but only by God the Creator, made known through Jesus."[1] If this is true, and I believe it is, then we must understand where a person's heart is if we are to fill that "God-shaped hole." If Jesus truly wants to come and live in our heart, what does that mean on a practical level? Where does He actually come and live?

In order to answer this important question, we have to go to the Bible. In the Old Testament and New Testament alike,

Hebrew and Greek words describing the *belly* or *bowels* are regularly translated "heart" in our English versions. For example, in John 7:38 in the New King James Version, the Greek word for *belly* is rendered as *heart*, but the King James Version provides a more literal translation: *"He that believeth on Me, as the scripture hath said, out of his belly shall flow rivers of living water."*

The Message says it this way: *"Rivers of living water will brim and spill out of the depths of anyone who believes in Me this way."* So the heart is described as residing in "the depths" of our being, or as David said, in the "innermost being" and "hidden part" of us (see Ps. 51:6). The Bible has a lot more to say about the location and function of the heart as well. Let's look at a few of these:

- The heart is the seat of our emotions.

  Whoso hath this world's good, and seeth his brother have need, and shutteth up his bowels of compassion from him, how dwelleth the love of God in him? (1 John 3:17 KJV)

- The door of the heart has the ability to open or shut.

  But whoever has this world's goods, and sees his brother in need, and shuts up his heart from him, how does the love of God abide in him? (1 John 3:17)

- The anointing of the Holy Spirit is released and flows from the heart; or as the King James Version puts it, from the belly.

  He who believes in Me, as the Scripture has said, out of his heart will flow rivers of living water (John 7:38).

Above all else, guard your heart, for it is the wellspring of life (Proverbs 4:23 NIV).

Whoever drinks of the water that I shall give him will never thirst. But the water that I shall give him will become in him a fountain of water springing up into everlasting life (John 4:14).

- Wounds of the heart are located in the belly as well.

The words of a talebearer are as wounds, and they go down into the innermost parts of the belly (Proverbs 18:8 KJV).

- And the spirit of man is said to reside in the belly or heart.

The spirit of man is the candle of the Lord, searching all the inward parts of the belly (Proverbs 20:27 KJV).

The spirit of a man is the lamp of the Lord, searching all the inner depths of his heart (Proverbs 20:27).

Within our heart, we locate the following:

- The seat of grief (see John 14:1; Rom. 9:2; 2 Cor. 2:4).
- Joy (see John 16:22; Eph. 5:19).
- The desires (see Matt. 5:28; 2 Pet. 2:14).
- The affections (see Luke 24:32; Acts 21:13).
- The perceptions (see John 12:40; Eph. 4:18).

- The thoughts (see Matt. 9:4; Heb. 4:12).

- The understanding (see Matt. 13:15; Rom. 1:21).

- The reasoning powers (see Mark 2:6; Luke 24:38).

- The imagination (see Luke 1:51).

- The conscience (see Acts 2:37; 1 John 3:20).

- The intentions (see Heb. 4:12; 1 Pet. 4:1).

- Purpose (see Acts 11:23; 2 Cor. 9:7).

- The will (see Rom. 6:17; Col. 3:15).

- And faith (see Mark 11:23; Rom. 10:10; Heb. 3:12).

In order to receive deep relief now, we need to understand the connections between the emotions and the belly, the belly and the heart, and the heart and the human spirit. God wants to release the anointing of His Spirit in our life, flowing to bring deep healing for ourselves and for others.

The Location of the Thoughts

Everyone seems to know where his or her thoughts are located. Whenever Dr. Jen and I speak to a group of people and ask them this question, they all instantly point to their head. There's no confusion on that one.

Thoughts are formed in the brain by recalling information stored in our memory, and by processing that information we are applying knowledge to make decisions and solve problems. The conscious mind is aware of only a fraction of brain activity at any given time. But our entire life story, every minute detail, is actually stored away in our subconscious mind.

We have all forgotten far more than we will ever remember. The truth is that when someone describes a crisis after the fact, they often say, "I saw my whole life pass before my eyes." This is because long-forgotten memories were retrieved and brought into conscious awareness once again.

It's important to realize that every thought we have has a corresponding emotion attached to it. Feeling nostalgic when we smell something connected with a pleasant childhood memory exemplifies this well. Something like freshly baked cookies or the evergreen smell of Christmas can bring back a flood of memories and emotions attached to those memories. I'm not saying this is only true with positive memories—it is true of both positive and negative ones.

Memories are stored as feeling-thought combinations. That's why some memories still make us feel sad and others stir up happy feelings deep within. But the thoughts that cause us the most trouble, of course, are those connected to negative emotions.

The Location of the Emotions

Most people associate their heart with their emotions. That's why Valentine's Day hearts are often associated with and mean love. But our heart, according to the way the Bible describes it, is the seat of the emotions,[2] the center of our inward life,[3] the hidden springs of our personality,[4] and the sphere of divine influence.[5] According to Scripture, then, our Bible heart is the center of our emotions (see Matt. 5:28; Luke 24:32; John 16:22; Eph. 5:19), and it resides in the belly.

In modern terminology, we talk about gut hunches, gut feelings, or gut reactions. Often people are told to "go with their gut" when making decisions. This means it generally works out better to listen to the heart in addition to the head, rather than the head alone. Our choices are usually wiser when they're based on more than just mental reasoning alone. This isn't to say that mental reasoning is bad by any means, but only that if we use our whole being to make decisions rather than one part of our person, then our decisions will often tend to be much better.

Think about it for a second. We wouldn't want to marry someone based solely on logical analysis, would we? It's doubtful that either person would be very happy in the long run if marriage came about that way. We, of course, use logical analysis, but there is also something much more taking place.

Emotions, the Gut, and Physical Health

As a child, we probably got "butterflies in our tummy" when we anticipated a special holiday, prepared for the first day of school, or found out our grandparents were getting us a special gift. Likewise, we've probably known about children who get tummy aches when they're emotionally distraught. They feel their emotional pain in their belly.

Medical researchers and health professionals have known for a long time that physical health is connected to emotional health. Negative emotions are harmful to the physical body. And because the gastrointestinal tract is so closely linked with emotions, negative emotions commonly disrupt the digestive organs or even lead to eating disorders.

Women suffer from irritable bowel syndrome and functional somatic disorders at least twice as often as men. These disorders are closely linked with anxiety, stress, and mood disorders, and they tend to weaken the immune system and increase inflammatory activity.[6]

But although eating disorders have commonly been considered a woman's complaint, new research has shown that more men struggle with eating disorders than previously believed. A recent Harvard study found that, out of 3,000 people suffering from bulimia and anorexia, 25 percent were male, and 40 percent of the men were binge eaters.[7]

The Gut Knows

Did you know that people have an emotional response if they tell a lie? That's what is actually measured indirectly by a polygraph (lie detector) test, as emotions trigger physiological responses in the body.

A polygraph measures involuntary responses in a person's body when he or she experiences the stress associated with deception. Through a combination of medical devices that monitor physiological changes, the examiner determines the normal level for that particular person. Then they check for variations in heart rate, blood pressure, respiratory rate, and sweatiness of the fingers, compared to normal levels.

Because some people learn to control these key responses through biofeedback, researchers have discovered what may be the ideal lie detector test. It measures gut responses and appears to be unbeatable. According to an article in *New Scientist* magazine:

> Truth may be found in the [gut], at least where lie detector tests are concerned. Pankaj Pasricha and colleagues at the Medical Branch of the University of Texas used an electrogastrogram to measure nerve activity in the stomachs of 16 volunteers when they were either lying or telling the truth. The team found a significant increase in activity when the volunteers were lying but no increase when they were telling the truth. "The gut has a mind of its own," says Pasricha. "Its nervous system acts independently." The work was presented...at the annual

scientific meeting [2005] of the American College of Gastroenterology.[8]

The Location of the Will

The Bible tells us that the center of choice and volition is in the heart. And we have already established that our Bible heart is in our belly. *Vine's Expository Dictionary* says the heart is also the seat of the conscience, intention, and will.[9] In the Old Testament, the Hebrew word for "reins" is sometimes used for the will. The literal translation for "reins" is kidneys, which locates the seat of our volition in the gut. Jeremiah said: *"I the Lord search the heart, I try the reins* [kidneys], *even to give every man according to his ways, and according to the fruit of his doings"* (Jer. 17:10 KJV).

Exerting our own willpower creates stress within our bodies. Willpower is the force of our own will trying to control our person, other people, or the circumstances of life. As soon as we feel tense or stressed, stress hormones are released throughout our body, and our muscles contract. Whenever we face a perceived threat, our body reacts by going into self-protection mode. But we feel it first in the gut.

If we pay attention the next time a minor inconvenience occurs, we'll notice that our muscles tighten in our gut. Although we might not realize it at the moment, we can learn to catch ourselves at this early stage and let it go. But if we continue to stay stressed, our muscular tension is likely to increase and spread to our back, shoulders, and neck.

When we are suspicious about someone's motives, we close our heart to that person. Our heart says, "No, I will not be vulnerable to that person." So our will opens and shuts the door of our heart. (Remember the "open and shutting" principle we pointed out in 1 John 3:17?) When we feel tension in our gut, it's a sign that our willpower has been engaged. However, when we pray and trust God's help, we open our heart to Him, and we automatically relax.

Practice: Here are some simple ways you can test out the "gut principle." Stand up and allow yourself to fall back a little, but stop yourself before you actually fall down. (You may want to stand with your back against a wall, or have someone stand behind you when you try this.) Where do you feel the stop? It is in the gut. You stopped yourself as an action of your will. Now close your eyes and think of an unpleasant person or a situation that stresses you out. Pay attention to what you sense in the gut when you think about it. Which would you rather live in?

Have you ever noticed the back belt worn by workers who lift heavy objects in the workplace? It wraps around the midsection and low back to support their spine and lower body. During times of stress, reflexive abdominal bracing occurs (imagine bracing yourself before a punch in the gut), signaling the abdominal muscles to tighten, functioning just like an internal back belt.

When someone tells us to "let it go," we can do that by releasing it from our gut. If we notice that we are becoming tense when we have a deadline coming up at school or at work, we can relax and let God help. But the secret is learning how to do it, and this all begins with knowing location, location, location.

Our inner distress is located in our heart—in our belly or gut—and that's where the relief must come from as well. In the following chapters, we'll learn more about the practical steps for receiving deep relief, and receiving it quickly.

ENDNOTES

1. Blaise Pascal wrote this in his book *Pensées.*

2. J. Strong, *Strong's Exhaustive Concordance of the Bible,* Hebrew and Chaldee Dictionary, lêb, #3820. (Nashville, TN: Thomas Nelson Publishers, 1990), 58.

3. W. E. Vine, *Vine's Expository Dictionary of Old and New Testament Words* (Fleming H. Revell Company, 1981), 297.

4. Ibid.

5. Ibid.

6. E. Goddard, K. Barth, and B. Lydiard, "Disorders Which Frequently Overlap With Irritable Bowel Syndrome: Can a Shared Neurobiology Explain Their Frequent Association?" *Primary Psychiatry,* 14(4), (1997), 69-73. D. Drossman, M. Camilleri, E. Mayer, and W. Whitehead, "AGA technical review on irritable bowel syndrome." *Gastroenterology,* 123(6), (2002), 2108-2131. G. Longstreth, W. Thompson, W. Chey, L. Houghton, F. Mearin, and R Spiller, "Functional bowel disorders," *Gastroenterology,* 130(5), (2006), 1480-1491. Erratum in: *Gastroenterology,* 31(2), 688. O. Palsson, and W. Whitehead, "Comorbidity associated with irritable bowel syndrome," *Psychiatric Annals,* 35(4), (2005), 320-324. L. Chang, "Neuroendocrine and neuroimmune markers in IBS, pathophysiology or epiphenomenon," *Gastroenterology,* 130(2), (2006), 596600. D. Drossman, "The functional gastrointestinal disorders and the Rome III process," *Gastroenterology,* 130(5), (2006), 1377-1390.

7. J. Hudson, E. Hiripi, H. G. Pope, and R. C. Kessler, "The Prevalence and Correlates of Eating Disorders in the National Comorbidity Survey Replication," *Biological Psychiatry,* 61(3), (2007), 348-358.

8. S. Hutson, "The stomach cannot lie," *New Scientist Magazine*, online edition, issue 2524, 2005. Retrieved January 6, 2010, from http://www.newscientist.com/article/dn8238.

9. W. E. Vine, *Vine's Expository Dictionary of Old and New Testament Words* (Fleming H. Revell Company, 1981), 297.

Chapter 7

LEARNING ANOTHER LANGUAGE

By Dr. Jen

Missing Keys

Before I met Dennis, my prayer life consisted mostly of talking to God and praying through prayer lists for the needs of other people or myself. I went to prayer meetings from time to time, and that seemed to be the way most people prayed. Sometimes I read books or took courses that included written prayers, and I prayed those too. I had also taken a number of courses on Christian counseling, and they often provided lists of prayers for healing the heart. But despite my best efforts to follow their suggested formulas, my own heart received only minimal healing.

This lack of true relief was frustrating to say the least, and I could tell I wasn't the only one experiencing it. I observed that most people who were wounded seemed to struggle for a long time with their emotional baggage, despite many hours of therapy or seminars. Their ongoing problems seemed to stem from an inability to forgive, even though they had tried to forgive for months or even years. My Christian counseling training also taught that forgiveness was a long process.

When Dennis started explaining the principles of deep relief now, it was like learning a whole new language. Although I considered myself well versed in both the Bible and psychology, I had somehow missed some fundamental keys for true healing of the heart.

Understanding the Heart's Door

The first lesson Dennis taught me was how to connect, commune, and communicate with God on an ongoing basis. That sounds simple enough, doesn't it? Yet I found that I'd been missing out on some revolutionary concepts.

Imagine hearing a car pull up to your house, and you see your least favorite person in the whole world heading down the path to your front door. What do we usually do? We oftentimes put up a wall in our heart, which is a typical response of the will to perceived danger. We are closing off our heart to protect ourselves from danger. It is a defense mechanism.

Whenever we get tense, our will is what tightens up. And when we are stressed, our willpower has taken over as we attempt to control ourselves, other people, or our circumstances.

Practice: Close your eyes and focus on your heart for a moment. Picture that person you don't want to encounter. Now pay attention to how it feels in your gut. Tense? Apprehensive? Angry? Like a wall? You certainly don't feel like flinging the door of your heart open to him or her, do you? Now picture a person you love. Perhaps your child, grandchild, or best

friend. Does your heart "soften" and feel more open
and positive? Take note of these different feelings.

Our heart has a door giving the Lord access to fill the God-shaped hole residing in our heart. Jesus says He stands at the door of our heart and knocks, waiting for us to open to Him. So we can choose, as an act of our will, whether or not we are going to open up to Him (see Rev. 3:20).

What I had always missed was that the same door we open for Jesus to come into our heart at salvation is the same door we must open for Him in our daily lives. It's like a "valve" that can open or shut off our spiritual connection with Him. It is not that we open the door for Him at salvation and then close it once He enters the house of our heart. Rather, it is the same door we open day after day after day, allowing Him access to us so He can bring deep and lasting healing to our emotional pain.

Jesus challenged the religious leaders of His day to this very same purpose:

> *You have your heads in your Bibles constantly because you think you'll find eternal life there. But you miss the forest for the trees. These Scriptures are all about Me! And here I am, standing right before you, and you aren't willing to receive from Me the life you say you want* (John 5:39-40 MSG).

For all their religious studies and efforts to please God, these leaders had missed the point. They couldn't see the forest for the trees. This could be said about many of us as well. We focus on the details but fail to grasp the big picture.

At the time of salvation, our spirit experiences a new birth, enabling us to connect with a heavenly realm that was inaccessible before. God is a spiritual being, and those who worship (acknowledge and honor) Him must approach Him in spirit and truth (the reality of who He is, the genuine instead of the counterfeit). Because of this, our connection with our heavenly Father must be made by our spirit rather than through our intellect.

Thinking about God is not the same as actually making a *connection* with Him. I love how The Message renders Jesus's words in John 4:23-24:

> *Your worship must engage your spirit in the pursuit of truth. That's the kind of people the Father is out looking for: those who are simply and honestly themselves before Him in their worship. God is sheer being itself—Spirit. Those who worship Him must do it out of their very being, their spirits, their true selves, in adoration.*

I encourage you to go back and read this passage one more time, letting it really sink in. Ask God to make this kind of intimacy with Him a reality in your life.

Dropping Down

When Dennis and I sat down to pray, he told me to close my eyes and focus on God. He explained that when believers pray, they automatically make a spirit-to-Spirit connection with God. Dennis taught me to "drop down" to Christ in my heart, which simply meant I needed to get out of my head (my intellect) and make an inner connection with Christ in my heart (my spirit).

As believers, we have an inner pipeline directly to the fountain of living waters. However, when we don't focus on our spiritual relationship with the Lord, it's like closing up the line with a shut-off valve. Instead of being just some kind of mystical theory, this has practical applications for our daily lives. A member of our church testified to me that she could "drop down," commune with the Lord, and stay in peace even while she was having dental work done.

In fact, one person wrote to us not long ago, explaining how they've learned to walk in continual peace: "Due to the ministry of Dennis and Dr. Jen Clark, my life as a Christian has been transformed. I used to experience lots of oppression and torment, and I lived out of my head instead of my heart. But after participating in Dennis and Dr. Jen's seminars, I've learned to walk in the Spirit, live out of the Spirit, and walk in continual peace and communion with the Lord. While most seminars and conferences are all about head knowledge, the Clarks do the experiential as well, so you learn to apply God's Word to real life."

We often have misconceptions that hinder our ability to apply the "drop down" principle. In my case, I had grown up believing I must pray to a God who was far, far away in heaven. Even though I knew I had invited Jesus to come into my heart, I still approached prayer as a long-distance call, which automatically created a feeling of separation between God and me. I later discovered that many others have the very same misconception.

Yet the Bible says we can know God personally and intimately, as our Immanuel, or "God with us": *"'They shall call His name Immanuel,' which is translated, 'God with us'"* (Matt. 1:23); He is *"Christ in you, the hope of glory"* (Col. 1:27); and *"the kingdom of God is within you"* (Luke 17:21). If we've given our heart to Christ, He isn't "way out there," but rather "right in here." Paul wrote about this vital truth in Romans 10:6-8:

> *The righteousness of faith speaks in this way, "Do not say in your heart, 'Who will ascend into heaven?'"*

> (that is, to bring Christ down from above) *or,*
> *"'Who will descend into the abyss?'"* (that is, to bring
> Christ up from the dead). *But what does it say?*
> *"The word is near you, in your mouth and in your*
> *heart"* (that is, the word of faith which we preach).

Christ will make His home in our hearts when we invite Him in. So there's no need for a long-distance call when we're talking to God. He is right there with us. As Paul prayed, *"Christ will live in you as you open the door and invite Him in"* (Eph. 3:16 MSG).

The Peace of Connecting with God

Whenever I made a connection with the Lord in prayer, Dennis told me to pay attention to how it felt. I noticed that I instantly felt a sense of peace. If I opened my eyes and started thinking about house repairs or all the reports I had to write for work, however, my peace changed into mild anxiety. Yet as soon as I went back to prayer, the anxiety left and I felt the same peace return again. My worries simply faded away.

I tried this exercise numerous times, and the result was always the same. When I focused on repairs or reports, the anxiety came back. But when I closed my eyes and made a prayer connection again, God's perfect peace returned. This shouldn't have really surprised me, for it's exactly what the Scriptures promise:

> *You will keep in perfect peace all who trust in You, all whose thoughts are fixed on You!* (Isaiah 26:3 NLT)
>
> *Don't worry about anything; instead, pray.... Then you will experience God's peace, which exceeds anything we can understand. His peace will guard your hearts and minds as you live in Christ Jesus* (Philippians 4:6-7 NLT).

Peace. Inner tranquility. Freedom from stress and fear. These verses say we can experience God's peace in the midst of *any* situation. But this has to go beyond memory verses—it must become a personal discovery for each and every one of us. What a joy it was to finally learn how to experience what God has promised in His Word all along. Every time I made a connection with Him in prayer, my internal conflict dissipated, and I felt deep peace inside.

Practice: Close your eyes and pray. Pay attention to Christ within, and be aware of how you feel inside. It will help you focus if you place your hand on your gut. Notice that there is a gentle perception of peace.

One of the biggest delights of a mother or father is hearing a child say, "Mama," or "Dada," for the very first time. Although a child is born with an ability to learn the language of his or her parents, the skill must be *learned*, and that takes time and practice.

In the same way, in my early days as a Christian, I had little confidence in my ability to hear from God. Of course, I believed He still communicated with humankind. But when He spoke to me personally, I often questioned, "Was that really God, or did I just imagine it?" I was still a novice at how to hear and understand the language of the Spirit.

I gradually learned a principle that really helped me, though, and I know it will help you too. Although God communicates to us in many different ways, His love nature is always attached to His voice. So no matter how He seems to be speaking to us, we can know it's truly Him if it's wrapped in love and faithful to His written Word.

The Language of Emotions

I learned from Dennis that the peace and joy I felt in prayer were manifestations of the love of God described in the fruit of the Spirit: *"The fruit of the Spirit is love, joy, peace, longsuffering, kindness, goodness, faithfulness, gentleness, self-control* [temperance]*"* (Gal. 5:22-23).

Have you ever felt joy in your child's achievement, compassion when they suffered a disappointment, or tender affection as you gazed upon their sleeping face? It's all the same love, but it comes in different expressions depending on the situation.

In the natural realm, there are two broad categories of emotions. Human emotions are either love based or fear based. Everyone likes to feel the love-based emotions. If we could pick just one emotion, most people would choose to be happy all the time. People dislike negative, fear-based emotions so much so that they spend a lot of time and effort trying to numb them through drugs, alcohol, or addictive behaviors.

Medical science has discovered that emotions play a major role in physical health. It is well documented that love-based emotions are good for the body, but fear-based emotions often lead to disease. They are not only toxic, but they're sometimes even deadly. In describing the traumatic events of the end times, Jesus says one of the signs will be *"men's hearts failing them from fear"* (Luke 21:26). How amazing that people can literally be scared to death.

God Emotions: The Fruit of the Spirit

In addition to love-based and fear-based emotions, the Bible says there's a third category of emotional experience available for believers: God emotions. The God emotions are even better than human, love-based emotions. Since they spring from God Himself, the Bible calls these emotions "the fruit of the Spirit" (see Gal. 5:22-23).

God is an emotional God. When we encounter the God who is love, it shouldn't surprise us that our emotions are impacted in a positive way. God doesn't just *have* love, He *is* love!

We are made in God's image (see Gen. 1:26-28). And just as we have human emotions, He has supernatural, God emotions. When we sense the love and presence of God, our emotions touch His emotions, and as that happens, we experience the love, joy, peace, and hope of God. This is why Paul said, *"May the God of hope fill you with all joy and peace as you trust in Him, so that you may overflow with hope by the power of the Holy Spirit"* (Rom. 15:13 NIV).

It's crucial to understand that this experience has nothing to do with human effort or a self-help program. When God's love is added into the mix, we experience supernatural love, joy, peace, and the other types of the fruit of the Spirit. That's why Jesus says His peace is much deeper than anything the world can give us:

> *Peace I leave with you, My peace I give to you; not as the world gives do I give to you. Let not your heart be troubled, neither let it be afraid* (John 14:27).

God's peace is the peace *"which surpasses all understanding,"* and it *"will guard your hearts and minds through Christ Jesus"* (Phil. 4:7). The word translated "understanding" here is the Greek word *nous*, which includes thoughts, choices, and emotions. God's supernatural peace is supremely better, higher, and more excellent than anything that comes from our human thinking, choosing, or feeling.

Hearing God's Voice

Have you ever questioned whether or not you're really able to hear from God? Jesus says four times in John 10 that His sheep can both hear and recognize His voice:

> *He who enters by the door is the shepherd of the sheep. To him the doorkeeper opens, and the sheep hear his voice; and he calls his own sheep by name and leads them out. And when he brings out his own sheep, he goes before them; and the sheep follow him, for they know his voice. Yet they will by no means follow a stranger, but will flee from him, for they do not know the voice of strangers.... And other sheep I have...and they will hear My voice.... My sheep hear My voice, and I know them, and they follow Me* (John 10:2-5,16,27).

Of course, it's possible to hear Him but not understand. A child hears parental voices even in the womb, but it takes a few years to understand everything that is said. Sometimes people can hear God's voice but not understand what He means. In John 12:28, God spoke from heaven and said, *"I have both glorified* [My name] *and will glorify it again."* The people who stood by could hear Him speak, but they just thought it had thundered.

God wants to speak to His people, and He wants us to understand His words. Here are some of the diverse ways He speaks to us:

- The Bible (see 2 Tim. 3:16; Ps. 119:11,105).
- The still small voice of the Holy Spirit (see Acts 16:6-7; 1 Kings 19:12-14).

- Creation and the world of nature (see Rom. 1:20).

- The audible voice of God (see Acts 9:4-5).

- Dreams and visions (see Matt. 1:20-21; Acts 10:9-18).

- Angels (see Luke 1:26-38; Acts 8:26).

- Circumstances and apparent coincidences (see Gen. 24:14-16).

- Inner assurance and peace (Rom. 8:16; Acts 27:10-13; Col. 3:15).

- People (see Acts 9:17).

- Revelation and illumination (see 2 Cor. 4:6; Eph. 3:3; Gal. 1:12).

- Our conscience (Rom. 2:15).

Learning God's Love Language

Children are meant to learn the language of their parents in an atmosphere of a loving relationship. Likewise, when a person wants to have a close relationship with someone from a different culture, they make an effort to learn their language and customs. In fact, researchers have found that even adults, who have a more difficult time mastering unfamiliar languages than children, learn a new language more easily if they fall in love with someone who speaks that language.

One thing we know for sure is that *"God is love"* (1 John 4:8), which means that whenever He speaks, love is automatically attached to His words. In the same way, love is the motivation behind all of His actions. And when we respond back to Him in love, it creates a mutual relationship in which we can discover the love language of God.

Have you ever realized that we notice something more if it's important to us? For example, if we are interested in purchasing a certain make and model of car, we begin to see similar cars everywhere on the road, although we never paid much attention to them before.

Dennis encouraged me to be aware of even the gentle whispers of the Holy Spirit while in prayer. I began to notice that the presence of God felt stronger at certain times than others. I also noticed that His presence seemed to decrease when I became distracted by a household chore or preoccupied with irrelevant thoughts. And when I read my Bible, I learned to linger over certain verses that were accompanied by an increased sense of His presence in my life.

I was gaining a keener perception of subtle changes in the spiritual atmosphere. As my spiritual awareness became more finely tuned, it was like learning a whole new language. Instead of being merely an academic exercise, this new discernment was a critical ingredient in experiencing deep relief and passing it on to others as well.

Chapter 8

LORD, TEACH ME TO PRAY

By Dr. Jen and Dennis

Radically Changed (Dr. Jen)

My prayer life radically changed as Dennis began teaching me how to pray. I had been making the mistake of praying to God, far away in heaven, but Dennis instructed me to focus on Christ within. Although I knew intellectually that I'd invited Jesus into my heart when I was saved, it was a new experience to learn what it means to open my heart and yield to Him moment by moment.

Dennis had developed keen discernment about God's presence, and he told me he could sense the Spirit's anointing as soon as I was in prayer. I learned to feel the difference, too, so I didn't have to just take his word for it.

Then Dennis gave me a helpful key for focusing on Christ within. He told me it would be easier to stay focused on my heart if I kept my hand on my belly. For a number of months, that suggestion really helped to keep my thoughts from wandering during prayer. Let me be clear here: this wasn't some kind of weird form of Eastern meditation. I didn't repeat any mantra or phrase over and over again, nor did I try to make my mind "blank." I simply became more aware of God and less distracted by my thoughts.

With Dennis's encouragement, I learned to linger in that place of prayer. I also discovered that the more I yielded to God, the more His presence increased. As I allowed Him to be in control of my being, I was increasingly able to sense His nearness. I was living out the cry of John the Baptist's heart when he said, *"He must increase, but I must decrease"* (John 3:30).

Practice: Try it yourself. Close your eyes in an attitude of prayer. Yield your heart to the Lord. How does it feel inside? What you are feeling can be described as having an "open" heart. Now open your eyes and think about unpleasant work situations or unfinished chores you have to do. How does that feel? Close your eyes and pray again. Pay attention to the difference.

Making the Heart Connection

One definition of prayer is simply spiritual communion. And another way to think of communion is by having a "heart connection" with someone, which is necessary for any true relationship to occur. Think about it for a moment. We cannot have a close relationship with someone unless we care about that person. When we're truly involved with another person relationally, we genuinely care for them. Hearts become *"knit together in love,"* as Paul describes in Colossians 2:2.

This "knitting" of hearts is why we use phrases like "bond of love," "bonding between mother and baby," or becoming "attached to someone." Communion implies connection, and connection takes place in the heart. Paul speaks of this when he says we should be *"endeavoring to keep the unity of the Spirit in the bond of peace"* (Eph. 4:3).

Love begins with emotional motivation accompanied by decision. The Bible says we have the ability to either open or shut the door to our hearts (see Rev. 3:20). Even though the context of Revelation is talking about opening and shutting our hearts to Jesus, it has further implications than that. When we are around another person, we can either open the door and connect with them or we can shut the door and detach from them.

Becoming an Openhearted Person

Many of us have heard the term *being openhearted*. But what does it mean? It means being a person who is emotionally open to people and the experiences taking place around us. It means that the door of our heart is open and we are emotionally available to others.

Paul points out to the believers in Corinth that his heart was open to them: *"O Corinthians! We have spoken openly to you, our heart is wide open"* (2 Cor. 6:11). In return, he requested the same openness from them: *"Open your hearts to us. We have wronged no one, we have corrupted no one, we have cheated no one"* (2 Cor. 7:2). Likewise, John writes of the open heart Christians should have toward those in need: *"Whoever has this world's goods, and sees his brother in need, and shuts up his heart from him, how does the love of God abide in him?"* (1 John 3:17).

As long as our heart remains open to God, we are in a state of prayer. If we are worried, stressed, angry, or preoccupied with the cares of life, then we have disconnected from God at that very moment. We've temporarily lost our intimate connection with Him and are trying to go at it alone.

Dennis taught me the amazing simplicity of prayer. No complicated formulas are needed, for prayer is simply communing with God. I learned to enjoy just being with the Lord and perceiving His presence. I didn't follow any system, but simply wanted a real relationship with a real God. While I sometimes asked God for specific requests, my overwhelming passion was to know Him better.

Simple prayer was the first and primary revelation I received from God during my times with Dennis. As intimacy in prayer was birthed, I found my inner pain and feelings of rejection being miraculously healed. I was in the early stages of experiencing what we've come to know as deep relief now.

A Passion to Know God

My times of prayer were not focused on "talking to God" any longer, but simply on experiencing His loving presence and enjoying fellowship with Him. I found that prayer didn't have to be a boring religious exercise or something just to cross off my daily to-do list. Instead, it became the most exhilarating and enjoyable part of my life. I actually looked forward to it.

Later, I read several books on prayer, but by that time I only had one, all-consuming prayer request: to know Him more. The books about prayer were confusing to me at first, because they focused almost entirely on petitioning God with our prayer requests. I became convinced that the approach I was learning from Dennis was much more satisfying, and that realization settled the question for me.

The passion of my heart was expressed in the words of the apostle Paul:

[For my determined purpose is] that I may know Him [that I may progressively become more deeply and intimately acquainted with Him, perceiving and recognizing and understanding the wonders of His Person more strongly and more clearly]... (Philippians 3:10 AMP).

I encourage you to stop for a minute right now and allow these words to sink deeply into your heart. Today can be the start of an exciting new beginning in your prayer life, enabling you to understand *"the wonders of His Person more strongly and clearly."*

Learning Intimate Prayer (Dennis)

After I had known the Lord for about 14 years, I felt that I already had a deep prayer life. Yet I sensed the Lord prompting me to request with new determination, "Teach me how to pray!" After this divinely initiated request, He began to lead me on a fantastic journey of inner transformation and greater intimacy with Him.

Jesus said, *"I am the vine, you are the branches. He who abides in Me, and I in him, bears much fruit; for without Me you can do nothing"* (John 15:5). Over a period of six months, the Lord wooed me closer to Him through a step-by-step process of abiding in prayer. I was then able to begin teaching these same Spirit-directed steps to others, later compiling them into seven distinct areas, or levels, of *intimate prayer*. God taught me these one at a time, staying on the same subject for several weeks or even months. Each step led me into greater intimacy and vulnerability in a loving, two-way relationship with Christ. What I call "simple prayer" is only the first of the seven levels of intimate prayer.

Every level of revelation about intimate prayer involved an inner work that allowed Him to search and purify my heart. As the Lord and I took this daily journey, He captured more and more of my heart, cleansing me of double-mindedness and impurity. I gained an acute awareness and sensitivity to His presence and the whisper of His Spirit.

This purification process wasn't always easy or pleasant, but it drew me closer and closer to the heart of God. I saw there was no other pathway to intimacy with Him, for Jesus taught us, *"Blessed are the pure in heart, for they shall see God"* (Matt. 5:8).

Prayer Steps

Are you ready to embark on your journey toward greater intimacy with God? You see, the key to experiencing deep relief now is not a matter of psychological formulas, but rather intimacy with our heavenly Father as a Person. For deep relief only comes through His presence, and His presence can only be experienced as we learn to continually abide in Him.

Simple prayer begins with coming before the Lord with anticipation, expecting to meet with Him and experience His presence. As we draw near to God, we present ourselves to Him as a living sacrifice, ready to yield to His Spirit and His voice (see Rom. 12:1-2).

Remember that we are coming to honor and adore God. As we come boldly before the throne of grace (see Heb. 4:16), we are to devote this time to seeking God for Himself alone. As we set out on our journey of simple prayer, it is not the time to petition for our own needs or intercede on behalf of others, although petitions and intercession are certainly important for a later stage.

As we enter more fully into His presence, we allow God to show us any sins in our life. We quickly receive His forgiveness and let Him wash and cleanse us with the water of His Word and the renewing of the Holy Spirit (see Titus 3:5). We don't condemn ourselves in the process, but rather yield to God's love.

It is important to not be in a hurry at this point. We must be willing to linger at each stage in the process for as long as it takes to turn each relational principle into a deep and lasting inner work. As we learn each lesson in vulnerability, dependence, and intimacy, He will teach us even more. But the attitude of our heart must be focused on the simplicity of pursuing a more intimate relationship with the Lord. This attitude of simplicity and humility is the good soil where the fruit of intimacy begins to flourish.

Undivided Attention

As we come to present ourselves before the Lord, there's an amazing fact we need to remember: He is giving us His undivided attention as we engage with Him. Whether we realize it or not, we are His constant delight: *"The Lord your God in your midst, the Mighty One, will save; He will rejoice over you with gladness, He will quiet you with His love, He will rejoice over you with singing"* (Zeph. 3:17). Every time we draw close to Him, it ravishes His heart because He loves us that much.

We must understand that He is right there with us, as close as the very air we breathe. It will do us well to think of this in the same way we would be aware of someone sitting in the back seat while we are driving our car. Although we can't always see the person, we know they are there with us, all the time. And just a quick glance in the rearview mirror confirms it.

When we focus on the Lord, His presence floods our mind, will, and emotions. As we focus on Him in this way, we can expect our surroundings to simply "slip away." We shouldn't be surprised if we're so caught up with Him that we lose a sense of time.

But in this process, we are likely to feel some initial resistance from our flesh. However, this will fade as we say no to distractions and stretch our capacity to remain in His presence a little longer each time. Small victories will enable us to develop power to overcome the flesh.

Four Touchstones to Remember

Simple prayer is simple. There are no complicated formulas to remember, nor any mantras to recite. As we progress in our journey, the principles will become second nature. We'll find ourselves instinctively responding to the Lord, with no need for confusion or struggle. But in the early phases of our journey in simple prayer, there are four important perspectives to be aware of.

Honoring God as a Person: As the Lord gives His full attention to us, we must acknowledge Him as a real Person who is present with us at all times. We must come before Him in reverence (see Heb. 12:28), recognizing the great privilege it is to have an audience with the King.

Listening to God: Listening is an awareness that includes the spiritual "inner knowings" of seeing, hearing, and touching. True listening means we gain an ever-increasing awareness and sensitivity to the Lord's presence and the promptings of His Spirit. This is a progressive lesson and is based on an unfolding discovery of who He is. We take the posture of a student before the Teacher, and we don't really have anything to say until we've first heard from Him (see Isa. 50:4).

Time spent with God: Just as natural growth takes time, spiritual growth requires time as well. Part of the journey toward simple prayer is learning to wait, and this is a necessary component in allowing God to heal and strengthen our heart. The psalmist said, *"Wait on the Lord; be of good courage, and He shall strengthen your heart*" (Ps. 27:14). As we become accustomed to being with the Lord, we will be able to stay in prayer for longer and longer periods of time. Rather than being religious drudgery, this will be our joy and delight.

Function and flow: The Gospels provide some powerful keys for how to function and flow in the Spirit, and we will cover these in-depth in a later chapter. For now, just remember that God has given us the spiritual capacity to receive from Him and release His *agape* love to others.

Constant Communing

I found that praying once or twice a day was one thing, but experiencing constant communion with God was quite another. This kind of communion is about maintaining our spiritual connection with the Lord all day long. We stop seeing our prayer times as being like stops at a gas station to fill our car up, for we are *continually* being filled with His presence.

Picture what it would be like to be married to someone, but to limit our time together to five- or ten-minute spans, once or twice a day. What if we made our spouse stand on the front porch the rest of the time, patiently waiting until we found a few minutes that were convenient for us to get together? Who would tolerate a relationship like that? Not anyone in their right mind. Yet, that's a pretty accurate picture of how many Christians treat their relationship with the Lord.

The Bible teaches God's design for marriage partners to be "one flesh" and describes the parallel with our spiritual intimacy with the Lord: *"He who is joined to the Lord is one spirit with Him"* (1 Cor. 6:17). Instead of being a sporadic on-again, off-again relationship, our communion with the Lord is meant to be 24 hours a day, 7 days a week, 365 days a year.

Dropping Down

Our mind is often one of the biggest barriers to the kind of spiritual communion I'm describing here. When Jen and I first started praying together, I often reminded her to focus on Jesus rather than on her own thoughts. We coined the phrase *drop down* to describe the need to stop thinking and start praying. In other words, our focus had to drop from our head to our heart.

Early in our marriage, we were driving together to Home Depot, and Jen's mind was agitated with thoughts of new flooring tiles, hardware to replace a doorknob, and similar concerns. Her mind raced with questions like, "Did I remember to bring the room dimensions?" and "Should I put up some extra shelves and make a pantry out of that closet?" Her inner peace evaporated.

I remember finally telling her, "Jen, you need to drop down." Instantly, she could make the prayer connection once again. Her thoughts stopped racing and her inner peace returned. She again experienced what Paul wrote about to the Colossians: *"Let the peace of God rule in your hearts"* (Col. 3:15).

Communion Defined

I've found that many people come from church backgrounds where the concept of "communion" in prayer is foreign. Others think I'm advocating some form of Eastern meditation, which is certainly not the case at all. In fact, what I'm advocating is something many Christians have experienced since the time of Jesus (remember Brother Lawrence?).

Communing is all about enjoying a mutual relationship with another person. It may be defined as having an intimate relationship or sharing thoughts and feelings with someone else. The Bible tells us that communion with the Lord and with other believers is meant to go beyond a mere intellectual or emotional relationship—it is *spiritual fellowship.*

In John 15:1-5, Jesus tells us to abide in Him, which means staying connected with Him in an ever-increasing way. He wants us to stay connected in spiritual fellowship with Him, and this means not just once in a while or every now and then. It doesn't even mean once a day during our scheduled "prayer time." It means that we are connected to Him *all* the time.

In the early days of our relationship, I remember encouraging Jen to keep growing in her relationship of communion with God. "Include Jesus in your life moment by moment," I told her. "Pay attention to the difference you feel when you connect with Jesus, not only in your prayer times, but also throughout the day." Although this wasn't easy for her at first, it eventually became a way of life.

In the Gospels, we learn that Jesus sometimes chose to be alone for prayer for extended periods of time. However, He was also in fellowship with His Father *all* of the time. He maintained a spiritual connection with Him throughout each and every day. Even amid jostling crowds in the noisy marketplace, Jesus was communing with Father God. John gives us a little insight into Jesus's constant communion with the Father:

> *Then Jesus answered and said to them, "Most assuredly, I say to you, the Son can do nothing of Himself, but what He sees the Father do..."* (John 5:19).

And,

> *Whatever I say is just what the Father has told Me to say* (John 12:50 NIV).

The apostle John gives us the wonderful news that we can have this same experience of communion with God. Of course,

John enjoyed a very close relationship with Jesus during His time on earth. But the relationship didn't end there. John writes that he was still having fellowship with Christ, and we can too.

> *From the very first day, we were there, taking it all in—we heard it with our own ears, saw it with our own eyes, verified it with our own hands. The Word of Life* (Jesus) *appeared right before our eyes; we saw it happen! And now we're telling you in most sober prose that what we witnessed was, incredibly, this: The infinite Life of God Himself took shape before us.*
>
> *We saw it, we heard it, and now we're telling you so you can experience it along with us, this experience of communion with the Father and His Son, Jesus Christ. Our motive for writing is simply this: We want you to enjoy this, too. Your joy will double our joy!* (1 John 1:2-4 MSG)

So if prayer is primarily about relationship, then we can stay in prayer as long as we maintain a connection, or communion, with Him. Even though we won't talk to God continuously, we *can* learn to stay plugged into Him throughout our daily routines. This means it's truly possible to abide with Him and *"pray without ceasing"* (1 Thess. 5:17). But it all begins with a passionate quest to know Him better and ask, "Lord, teach me to pray" (see Luke 11:1).

Simple prayer is the foundational ingredient for experiencing deep relief now. We are now ready for the next section of the book, on how healing prayer can quickly relieve our emotional pain. Are you ready?

Part Three

HEALING PRAYER

Interlude

HEALING EMOTIONAL PAIN

By Dennis

In this section on healing prayer we are going to deal with emotional pain, and also how to remove the obstructions—every impulse, thought, and emotion—that are hindering us from a far deeper union with God. Now that we're enjoying abiding with God through simple prayer, the goal here is that we all experience deep and lasting emotional healing in our relationship with Him.

Unresolved Issues

Each one of us have unresolved thoughts, feelings, and impulses that seem to come right out of the blue at all the wrong times. But through healing prayer, we are learning about letting God take these unresolved issues—these things that are hidden in the depths of our hearts and are springing up, causing ungodly thoughts, emotional outbursts of different types, and impulsive and destructive behaviors—and healing them. They are toxic expressions lying just under the surface of our hearts.

So even though we may be enjoying a peaceful union and communion with God in our lives, none of us have arrived yet, and we all have areas in our heart that conflict with enjoying the progressive intimate relationship we have with Christ. As we experience emotional healing, walking in the Spirit becomes less and less hindered by these intruders. We must learn to intentionally welcome God's presence so we move beyond just enjoying His presence in a place of a peace to diligently pursuing Him for deep healing.

The most effective way to diligently pursue God is not by telling Him we only want to enjoy intimacy with Him, but also by letting Him know we want Him to search our hearts. We long for Him to search out the hidden things deep with us, the affected areas that are buried alive under the surface of our hearts. And when He reveals what needs healing, then we're going to deal with whatever He exposes according to His process.

That's the diligent pursuit I'm talking about, because we all want these issues resolved in our life. These toxic expressions periodically paralyze us, periodically cost us in relationships and in many of the endeavors of our life. The Lord taught me how to instantly deal with issues such as these and get my peace back. Therefore, we need to passionately pursue this season of emotional healing, this area of intentional sanctification.

The psalmist prayed, *"Search me, O God, and know my heart; try me, and know my anxieties; and see if there is any wicked way in me, and lead me in the way everlasting"* (Ps. 139:23-24). It's not just about thinking this in our minds, but it's about allowing God to search our hearts through prayer. He is able to go right to the core of some of these barriers, the heart of the things that have hindered us, the issues that rise up and resurrect themselves, causing us trouble, and He is able to bring deep healing.

We're deliberately asking God to deal with these issues before they come up without notice. We are asking Him in advance to reveal the hidden areas of our hearts, allowing us to dismantle and abolish their effect in our lives. He longs for us to be free from the influence of these negative thoughts, impulses, and emotions. And we want to be those who respond rather than react—that's the goal of maturing in the things of God.

God-Tools

As we diligently pursue healing prayer, then God will reveal to us our God-tools, the tools that have been fitted within our heart, our capacity through prayer to tear down barriers that have been erected against the knowledge of God. We want every loose thought and emotion and impulse to be conformed into a structure of a life that is shaped by Christ. These tools are ready at hand for clearing the ground of every obstruction so that we can build a life of obedience unto maturity. That, again, is our diligent pursuit.

This God-tool of forgiveness is what removes the barrier at salvation and in our walk with God. We have a command that just as we received Christ, so we're to walk in Him (see Col. 2:6). When we received Christ in our beautiful conversion experience, it changed the way we thought, it changed the way we felt, it changed some of the choices we made, and it impacted all three areas of our being—spirit, soul, and body. And if that happened at conversion, how much more should we continue to walk in Him just as we received Him? Continually being transformed in our thoughts, emotions, and actions into a structure of a life that's being shaped by Him is what God desires for us (and what we should desire of Him). By His Word and by His Spirit we're being conformed more and more into His likeness.

There are some basic principles of forgiveness we need to understand and implement if we are to truly experience healing prayer. Probably the most important is that forgiveness deals with our own heart first. It doesn't mean we have to do something, like write a letter or go talk to a person (unless the Lord says to do such a thing). But the key principle of forgiveness is recognizing that it is something we deal with in our own heart. We must forgive from the heart, not from the head.

And the second principle is that Christ is the forgiver, so forgiveness works every time. Because Christ the forgiver in us is going to the area that needs healing—that barrier, hurt, or wound—He takes it away captive and washes it out. Forgiveness is instant, not a process. This is because He walks through the barriers—He never gets stuck. There are no big or little issues to forgive; it's all easy for Christ the forgiver who lives inside of us.

Sequence is important here, as we'll see throughout this section—we always go in God's order. As He searches our heart, we just become willing to deal with whatever comes to mind in each and every situation. We only allow ourselves to pray one thing at a time. Once we feel His peace in that particular area, that is an inner indication that the negative emotions are gone and His presence has replaced them—a supernatural exchange has taken place. Once that happens, then we're able to go on to the next issue.

It is my prayer as we move through this section that we allow God to search us, bringing deep relief now to all of our hurts and pains.

Chapter 9

WHAT MUST I DO TO BE SAVED?

By Dr. Jen

Elusive Freedom

Have you ever struggled in your Christian life? I sure did for many years. Everything seemed too hard, took too long, or simply just didn't work. I remember one preacher saying to take a piece of paper, write down a problem, then crumple it up and stomp on it. Well, I did what he said, but nothing changed in my life. I still had the same problem and a crumpled-up piece of paper.

Once I tried to forgive someone. Well, to tell you the truth, I not only tried, but I tried and tried and tried—yet I continued to hurt inside. I confessed forgiveness, cried about forgiveness, and even wrote and signed a forgiveness prayer in my journal. When none of those things relieved my distress, I sought prayer during altar calls, read countless books, and claimed every Bible promise that seemed to apply to me and my situation.

For some reason, true freedom was elusive. The festering sore in my heart wouldn't go away. I knew I must be missing something, but I couldn't figure out what it was. (What a mystery it was.) But when I met Dennis and began learning what the Lord had taught him about forgiveness, the answers were so simple. How had I overlooked them for this long? I had believed well-meaning but erroneous church teachings and faulty paradigms of my own.

In order to experience true forgiveness and deep relief, I had to learn a brand-new perspective and think outside the box. It became a season of reeducation for me, a time to learn new things and unlearn old ones. Everything Dennis taught me was extraordinarily simple yet so profound.

This new approach to Christian living was stated in a nutshell by the apostle Paul: *"So then, just as you received Christ Jesus as Lord, continue to live in Him"* (Col. 2:6 NIV). Simply put, as believers we must *continue* living in Christ in the *same way* we received Him at our initial salvation. I'm sure we all remember how we got saved. Well, Paul says the key to living the Christian life was given to us at the very first moment of our salvation. Let me explain what I mean.

Belief and the Emotional Heart

In contrast with the head, what characteristics do we normally associate with the word *heart*? The physical heart pumps our blood, and this action is necessary to keep our body supplied with oxygen and nourishment. But Scripture tells us that our spiritual heart supplies us with spiritual life, or *zoë*: *"For God so loved the world, that He gave His only begotten Son, that whosoever believeth in Him should not perish, but have everlasting life* (zoë)*"* (John 3:16 KJV).

The Bible says we must *believe* in our hearts (see Rom. 10:9-10) to connect with God's *zoë* life, and the heart is emotional. That means that salvation must include emotions. Love, Valentine's Day, broken hearts, openhearted—all of these have to do with our emotions, relationships, or the romantic life (which is associated with the heart). We cannot have a real relationship that doesn't include our emotions.

Jesus said, *"As the Father loved Me, I also have loved you; abide in My love"* (John 15:9). And the apostle John reminds us, *"Beloved, let us love one another, for love is of God; and everyone who loves is born of God and knows God. He who does not love does not know God, for God is love"* (1 John 4:7-8).

Sometimes the head and the heart can be in conflict with one another. If our thinking is twisted by carnal reasoning, it can cause us to ignore an important "gut hunch" the Lord wants us to pay attention to. (On the other hand, carnal emotions can lead us to make bad decisions.) So it's possible to think, speak, or do one thing, while our heart is saying just the opposite. Consider Jesus's correction to the Pharisees:

> *[Jesus] answered and said to them, "Well did Isaiah prophesy of you hypocrites, as it is written: 'This people honors Me with their lips, but their heart is far from Me'"* (Mark 7:6).

Opening Our Heart's Door

When we were born again, did we ask Jesus into our head, or into our heart? Most people laugh when they are asked that question. Believers seem to intuitively understand that they welcomed Jesus into their hearts when they were born again. Why is this important? Because belief in Jesus is relational, or emotional. Real relationship always involves making an *emotional* connection with the one we're in relationship with. We must open our heart to *care* about a person.

Paul explains it this way:

> *If you acknowledge and confess with your lips that Jesus is Lord and in your heart believe (adhere to, trust in, and rely on the truth) that God raised Him from the dead, you will be saved. For with the heart a person believes (adheres to, trusts in, and relies on Christ) and so is justified (declared righteous, acceptable to God), and with the mouth he confesses (declares openly and speaks out freely his faith) and confirms [his] salvation* (Romans 10:9-10 AMP).

There is an emotional door in our heart. That is what the term *openhearted* means—there's a door in our heart that can be opened or shut, allowing an emotional connection to take place between two people. When we open that door to God, we make a heaven connection (see Rev. 3:20). Therefore, the Bible says we must believe in our heart in order to be saved. This is how we entered into God's kingdom and the Christian life: we believed and opened our heart to Him.

It's not enough to merely agree with the Bible in a philosophical way. Believing that Jesus was a good man and that His teachings are admirable is mental assent, not saving faith. So we must welcome Him as our Lord and Savior, both personally and individually.

The Other Steps of Salvation

If we can open something, then by logical conclusion, it also means we can close it. When we open the door in our heart to

God, we instantly make a heaven connection and are no longer separated from the Lord. However, if we close the door, whether intentionally or inadvertently, we cut off our fellowship with Him.

In addition to opening our heart, there are two other notable parts of our initial salvation experience: we asked Jesus for forgiveness and we experienced peace with God. This was not just earthly peace, but the supernatural peace that *"surpasses all understanding"* (Phil. 4:7).

Just as these three words—open, forgiveness, and the fruit of peace—were key characteristics of our conversion experience, they are likewise the keys to walking in a victorious life in Him. Remember Paul's words once again: *"As you have therefore received Christ...[so] walk (regulate your lives and conduct yourselves) in union with and conformity to Him"* (Col. 2:6 AMP).

So if we're supposed to live in Christ in the same way as we received Him initially, what does that mean? How did we receive Christ when we were first saved? The steps in salvation, which I've greatly simplified here, are:

- Open: we opened the door of our heart and invited Jesus to come in.

- Forgiveness: we acknowledged that we were a sinner, received forgiveness, and were cleansed of our sins.

- Fruit: we instantly experienced an amazing and supernatural sense of peace (see Rom. 5:1).

Let's take a deeper look at how these steps apply to our ongoing relationship with the Lord.

Peace with God

When we opened the door of our heart to Jesus, we became emotionally available to Him. Then we received His gift of forgiveness and experienced peace with God. In order to open our heart to Jesus, however, we had to let down our guard and allow ourselves to trust Him. This meant becoming vulnerable with Him. But the reason we put up the walls in the first place was to protect our hearts so we wouldn't get hurt. Walls are an inner resistance based in fear and suspicion.

When Dennis and I started praying together, I realized I sensed a deep peace whenever I was in prayer. I could get anxious about home repairs, but as soon as I prayed and gave it all to God, the anxiety quickly changed to peace. It is important to remember that peace is not just the absence of external conflict. Even if two countries are not engaging in active warfare, when the inhabitants have hostility toward each other, they are not truly at peace. Likewise, if two people are courteous in public but are belligerent deep in their hearts, they are certainly not at peace with one another. Their words and gestures may hide their internal war, but they are at war nonetheless.

In a practical sense, peace is an emotion we feel. It is experienced as an absence of inner turmoil and the presence of deep calmness. Paul describes this as one of the first signs of our salvation:

> *Therefore, since we are justified (acquitted, declared righteous, and given a right standing with God) through faith, let us [grasp the fact that we] have [the peace of reconciliation to hold and to enjoy] peace with God through our Lord Jesus Christ (the Messiah, the Anointed One)* (Romans 5:1 AMP).

So if this incredible peace is a mark of our initial salvation experience, what does it take to maintain our peace as a part of our moment-by-moment relationship with the Lord? One of the clues is to recognize that peace is one of the "God emotions" available as a fruit of the Holy Spirit.

Fruit of the Spirit

I remember Sunday school lessons on the fruit of the Spirit when I was a child, but it always remained a mystery to me. Often we were told that the fruit required a choice to submit our lives to God, but we shouldn't expect to feel anything. I once went to a women's conference on joy, yet nobody there seemed to have any joy or know how to get it. This seemed very strange to me. I understood the principle of accepting God's blessings by *faith*, but shouldn't we *experience* something too?

When I was saved, I was thrilled with Jesus and the new life He had given to me. I knew this was more than just a mental concept. I was truly different inside, and everyone told me how much I had changed. Something brand-new had happened in my heart, and I felt much more secure and peaceful. I overflowed with all kinds of good emotions, just as Paul prayed the Christians in Rome would experience:

> *I pray that God, the source of hope, will fill you completely with joy and peace because you trust in Him. Then you will overflow with confident hope through the power of the Holy Spirit* (Romans 15:13 NLT).

You see, God Himself experiences emotions. He's not just a stoic, emotionless cosmic force—He feels love, anger, and pain.

That's why the Bible speaks of both *"the joy of the Lord"* (Neh. 8:10) and *"the wrath of God"* (Rom. 1:18).

Likewise, we see Jesus's emotions when He stood before the tomb of His friend Lazarus and was surrounded by the grieving siblings, Mary and Martha. John tells us that *"Jesus wept"* (John 11:35). And we see His anger when He removed the moneychangers from the temple (see John 2:14-17). Even after Jesus's death, resurrection, and ascension, we see Him as a High Priest who is *"touched with the feeling of our infirmities"* (Heb. 4:15 KJV).

In many ways, the fruit of the Spirit Paul describes in Galatians 5:22-23 are "God emotions"—the emotions the Holy Spirit wants to replicate in the lives of His people. God transforms our entire being through the process of sanctification, which is the ongoing practical experience of being set apart for God's work and being molded into the image of Christ.

Transformation primarily occurs through the renewing of the mind (see Rom. 12:2). However, the word Paul uses for "mind" is *nous* in the Greek, which refers to our thoughts, will, and emotions. Our thinking is changed by revelation from God, our will yields to God's will, and our carnal emotions are transformed by the fruit of the Spirit. Paul says:

> *And do not be conformed to this world, but be transformed by the renewing of your mind* (thoughts, will, and emotions)*, that you may prove what is that good and acceptable and perfect will of God* (Romans 12:2).

A Gateway to Knowing God

While it's no doubt true that people are sometimes deceived and led astray by unsanctified emotions, it's also true that God wants to redeem our emotions because they are a part of *us*. He wants our emotions to resonate with the God emotions of His Spirit because we are a people created in His image.

Jonathan Edwards (1703–1758) was a preacher, theologian, missionary to Native Americans, and the father of the First Great Awakening in America (1730–1760). Contrary to the views of many people of his day, Edwards said that the emotions are the gateway to knowing God. One couldn't truly know God unless his or her emotions were deeply impacted.

Nowhere is this plainer than in his 1746 text, *A Treatise Concerning Religious Affections*. It was penned at a time of great controversy during the First Great Awakening. Many clergymen objected to the emotional displays of those overwhelmed by spiritual experiences, so Edwards wrote a defense of heart-versus-head Christianity—emotional versus intellectual. According to Edwards, if the heart was not deeply affected, no true conversion had taken place nor was any spiritual transformation evident in an individual's life. Mental assent alone, therefore, was inconsequential for true belief.[1]

Commenting on 1 Peter 1:8 (KJV)—*"Whom having not seen, ye love; in whom, though now you see Him not, yet believing, ye rejoice with joy unspeakable and full of glory"*—he writes, "The proposition, or doctrine, that I would raise from these words, is this: ...True religion, in great part, consists in holy affections."[2] He went on to explain that the affections are "the most vigorous and sensible exercises of the inclination and will of the soul."[3] Inclination, as defined by Edwards, is emotional preference or aversion to a particular thing—but at its core, it is emotional nonetheless. And inclination was simply "liking or disliking, [being] pleased or displeased, [or] approving or rejecting."[4] So even though he was perhaps one of America's greatest thinkers, he realized the emotions played a vital role in one's relationship with the Lord.

Then why are many believers today so reluctant to allow the Lord to work through their emotions? Jesus didn't preach a merely cerebral faith, but rather told His disciples that they should expect to experience His peace, not just know about it with their minds. He said, *"Peace I leave with you, My peace I give to you; not as the world gives do I give to you. Let not your heart be troubled, neither let it be afraid"* (John 14:27).

While writing to the Philippians from a jail cell, Paul used the words *joy* or *rejoice* 18 times in only 104 verses. In addition to telling the believers in Philippi to rejoice always, he exhorted them to also be content and free from anxiety:

> *Rejoice in the Lord always. Again I will say, rejoice!... Be anxious for nothing, but in everything by prayer and supplication, with thanksgiving, let your requests be made known to God; and the peace of God, which surpasses all understanding, will guard your hearts and minds through Christ Jesus* (Philippians 4:4,6-7).

Paul is describing a special kind of peace, available only through an intimate, abiding relationship with Christ. This amazing, supernatural peace, Paul said, is better than our rational understanding, and it will guard and protect our *"hearts and minds."*

God loves us so much that He doesn't want us to live in fear or torment. He sent His Son to come and rescue us from the kingdom of fear and bring us into the kingdom of love. Even while we were still sinners, Jesus came to die for us and set us free. This is exactly what the Bible affirms as well:

[God] has delivered us from the power of darkness and conveyed us into the kingdom of the Son of His love (Colossians 1:13).

You did not receive the spirit of bondage again to fear, but you received the Spirit of adoption by whom we cry out, "Abba, Father" (Romans 8:15).

Inasmuch then as the children have partaken of flesh and blood, He Himself likewise shared in the same, that through death He might destroy him who had the power of death, that is, the devil, and release those who through fear of death were all their lifetime subject to bondage (Hebrews 2:14-15).

The encouraging message of these verses is clear: we don't have to live in fear or torment any longer. We can be set free from them and live with a deep and abiding relief.

The Fruit of Love

The love described in 1 Corinthians 13 is love springing from the very heart of our Father God. Every manifestation of the fruit of the Spirit is just a different expression of God's love: *"But the fruit of the Spirit is love, joy, peace, longsuffering, gentleness, goodness, faith, meekness, temperance: against such there is no law"* (Gal. 5:22-23 KJV).

Picture for a moment pure white light shining through a prism. As the prism separates the white light into a spectrum of colors, the colors of the rainbow are revealed. After passing through the prism, it's the same white light, but the different wavelengths contained within it are made visible.

Jesus refers to Himself as *"the light of the world"* (John 8:12). The Bible describes a rainbow—multicolored rays of light—surrounding the throne room in heaven (see Rev. 4:3). The pure light of His presence is refracted into all the colors of the rainbow, and even more than those colors. In a similar way, God's love is refracted into all the various forms of the fruit of the Spirit. No wonder Paul says, *"Love is the fulfillment of the law"* (Rom. 13:10). If we walk in God's love, all of His other commandments are kept.

God's Love for You

For many people, God's love is merely a doctrine or a memory verse. They can recite John 3:16 about God loving the world, but this has never become their personal experience. But what about you? Have you opened the door of your heart to the Lord—not just at your salvation, but also in your daily relationship with Him since then?

God's heart for relationship is revealed in the parable of the prodigal son (see Luke 15:11-32). The father grieved when his son was gone, and he rejoiced when his son came to his senses and returned home. However, through it all, the father loved his son and yearned for a close relationship with him—for him to return. The father (who represents the heavenly Father) was watching so intently that he saw his son even while he was quite a distance away from home. Filled with love and joy, he forgot both decorum and age as he ran to greet and embrace his child: *"While he was still a long way off, his father saw him and was filled with compassion for him; he ran to his son, threw his arms around him and kissed him"* (Luke 15:20 NIV).

God is waiting for us to draw even one step nearer to Him, and He will have compassion and run toward us. He wants us to be at peace with Him, experiencing a peace that surpasses our understanding.

But perhaps we're not like the younger son in the story—we might be more like his older brother. Both sons were estranged from their father, but we don't see that until the end of the story, when the older son refuses to enter the father's house and celebrate his brother's return (see Luke 15:28). How sad. The older brother allowed an offense to keep him from opening the door and participating in the party. As wonderful as it is to be saved, God also wants us to experience the joy of our salvation (see Ps. 51:12). He wants us to *"have and enjoy life, and have it in abundance"* (John 10:10 AMP).

What must we do to be saved and then live an abundant life *after* we are saved? God has already made provision for everything we need. All we have to do is open our heart, receive forgiveness, and experience His deep and abiding peace. And how do we walk in the Spirit then? It really isn't hard or complicated. We simply open the door of our heart and include Jesus in the moment, receive forgiveness, allowing our negative emotions to be instantly washed out, and then receive peace as soon as we forgive.

Notice that forgiveness is the step between being open and receiving peace. If we don't know how to apply forgiveness in daily life, then a walk in the Spirit will be both mysterious and elusive.

ENDNOTES

1.   Jonathan Edwards, *A Treatise Concerning Religious Affections* (New York: Cosimo Classics, 2007). The back cover of this edition sums up his main arguments throughout: "How do we discern between true religion, and false? In this classic treatise on the nature of authentic faith, enormously influential American preacher and theologian Jonathan Edwards (1703–1758) explores the difference between true and counterfeit religious experiences, and how deep and sincere emotion can accentuate a real connection to God."

2.   Jonathan Edwards, *A Treatise Concerning Religious Affections* (New York: Cosimo Classics, 2007), 9,23.

3.   Ibid., 24

4.   Ibid., 24

Chapter 10

CHRIST THE FORGIVER

By Dr. Jen

It Really Works

It's important for us to understand that the principles of deep relief now are not just a nice theory—they really work. And they work for people like you and people like me. Countless lives have already been transformed through the process, and you can be next. Here are a few testimonies of people who have received deep and lasting relief through God's presence.

Instant Recovery from Betrayal

After a trusted friend betrayed him, Rob lived with a continual undercurrent of resentment in his heart. Every time he thought about the other person, he got angry. Time and time again, Rob had said, "I forgive him"—but he remained a captive to his anger nevertheless. No matter how hard he tried, he couldn't shake his inner torment.

When Rob met with us, Dennis taught him how to use the how-to tools. In just a few short minutes, years of frustration and anger were replaced by a deep inner peace. The constant emotional gnawing in his gut vanished and, as a bonus, he was instantly healed of irritable bowel syndrome (IBS)!

A Rape Victim Finds Relief

Candice could hardly remember life without inner pain. Since childhood, it had been her cruel daily tormentor. More than 50 years before, when she was a young child living in Germany, Nazi soldiers had raped her. Her mother had warned her to stay away from them, but she had been disobedient. And the guilt of disobeying her mother only compounded her deep feelings of shame.

We prayed with Candice, and her agony was gone in under five minutes. Blown away by the rapid and complete relief from anguish and self-incrimination, Candice exclaimed, "That was too easy!" Yet her pain was completely gone—and gone permanently. The following day she told us she felt like a brand-new person, clean and whole. Incredulous, she said, "After being tormented my entire life, now I am free!"

Now I Can Feel God's Love for Me

In one of our meetings, the awesome sense of the presence and peace of God was incredibly strong. Attendees sat still for hours in the Lord's presence. Some slid out of their chairs and stretched out on the floor. Even small children who ordinarily were rambunctious remained still and attentive.

Dennis was sitting on the platform steps, and a woman came and sat down beside him. She told him in frustration, "I can't feel anything at all! All these other people seem to be experiencing God, but I feel nothing."

Dennis led her through some simple how-tos in prayer. She had been angry at God for allowing a particular circumstance to happen in her life, but now she was finally able to let it go.

Suddenly, she gasped. She could immediately feel a strong sense of God's presence. "Oh, this is wonderful...amazing!" she exclaimed. "Now I can feel God's love for me! He's telling me how much He loves me and is pouring His love right into my heart!"

She later thanked us, testifying that she was no longer suffering with depression or colitis. Best of all, she felt much closer to the Lord.

Deep Relief for a Divorced Pastor

A team of ministers traveled to Saltillo, Mexico, for a series of meetings with a few hundred Mexican pastors. When members of the team discovered that a pastor was in need of some private ministry, they asked Dennis if he would miss one of the services so he could pray with him.

The pastor told Dennis his heartbreaking story. He had married a beautiful woman who pretended to be a Christian but had a hidden agenda to sway him from the Lord. When she discovered he wouldn't renounce his beliefs and his pastoral calling, she divorced him. The whole experience left him devastated—feeling betrayed, wounded, and angry with her and with himself. He felt humiliated that he had such little discernment and allowed himself to be tricked in this way.

The man was part of a denomination that refused to allow divorced people to serve as pastors. The divorce was bad enough, but now he was faced with an overwhelming new layer of rejection and confusion. His ministry—and his entire future—seemed to be in doubt.

One step at a time, Dennis prayed with him until he went from emotional turmoil to a strong sense of inner peace. His hopelessness and despair were quickly replaced by new hope and joy.

A pastor's wife had sat in during Dennis's prayer time with this man. Although she and her husband were in ministry and had grown up in the church, she had never seen anything like this before. Dennis had led this troubled man to deep relief through steps that were simple, fast, and thorough. Amazed by how well this approach worked, she exclaimed, "Where did you learn to do this?"

God's Love Flooded His Heart

A man on staff at a Massachusetts church had struggled to forgive his father for years of rejection and neglect. He never felt like his father loved him or had been there for him. Although his father had not been physically absent from the home, he had been emotionally absent in his heart.

Dennis coached him through the steps of prayer. As soon as he felt the pain and anger leave, his perception changed and new clarity came. "Now I see why he couldn't love me like I wanted him to," the man exclaimed. "My father never received love himself when he was growing up!"

Instead of the wretchedness of his own pain, he suddenly felt deep compassion for his father. When he released his father from an internal demand for love, he instantly experienced God's love flooding into his heart for the first time.

Relief from His Father's Caustic Words

Phil volunteered to receive prayer ministry in front of a whole conference when we were teaching one time—on the microphone. He prayed with Dennis through a number of painful situations, and then suddenly hit the "big one." He remembered the time his Little League baseball team lost because he had struck out in the final inning.

His father humiliated him, calling him an idiot in front of the whole team. His father told him he would never amount to anything, and those painful words had stuck in Phil's brain ever since. As Dennis led him in a few minutes of prayer, he finally allowed God's love to fill the aching hole inside him. The deep torment was replaced by deep peace. His father's caustic words had lost their power over him and he was free at last.

Rob, Candice, and Phil (as well as a multitude of others mentioned above) found deep relief, and they found it quickly and permanently. In all of the above cases, forgiveness was one of the keys that set them free from their prison of torment. Let us look at the concept of forgiveness and what it means for our daily lives.

Misconceptions about Forgiveness

If we've spent any significant time around churches, then we've no doubt heard a lot about forgiveness. Yet why is it so difficult and confusing for most of us? We try to forgive, choose to forgive, and even pray to have strength to forgive—yet our unforgiveness and bitterness often remain.

One of the problems is that there are many misconceptions about forgiveness. Here are three of the most common:

- "If I forgive someone, it lets them off the hook for the harm they've done to me." But this is not the truth. The perpetrator must still answer to God after we forgive them, and sometimes they must also suffer legal penalties for their actions.

- The second misconception is, "If I forgive someone, I must allow them back into my life." Even though God holds us responsible to forgive those who have wronged us, we still must use wisdom and maintain appropriate boundaries in our relationships with those individuals.

- "Forgiveness is necessary for the big emotional traumas, but it's not required for small offenses." The truth is that even small fears, offenses, and hurt feelings can fester and cause ongoing emotional, relational, and physical harm if not dealt with properly.

Before we continue, we should take a few moments to pray and ask the Lord to show us if we've unwittingly adopted any of these misguided views about forgiveness. We should ask Him to show us the truth about how they have negatively impacted our life.

Christ the Forgiver

Christ is the forgiver. Jesus forgave us, He gave us the gift of forgiveness, and we forgive others by His grace that works in us. Christ the forgiver does all the work in and through us. We simply allow Him to forgive through us, thus releasing His forgiveness to others and ourselves. The Bible has many wonderful things to say about forgiveness:

> *I, even I, am He who blots out your transgressions for My own sake; and I will not remember your sins* (Isaiah 43:25).

> *In Him we have redemption through His blood, the forgiveness of sins, according to the riches of His grace* (Ephesians 1:7).

> *Even as Christ forgave you, so you also must do* (Colossians 3:13).

You must right now forgive our sins for us, in the same manner as we have completed forgiving everyone of everything, big and little, against us (Matthew 6:12 PNT).

One of the reasons we fail in our pursuit to live a lifestyle of forgiveness is that we don't know what forgiveness actually is and is not. Forgiveness is not releasing someone from their responsibility, being a doormat, removing the consequences of someone's actions, or absolving someone's sin while pretending to forget. Forgiveness is not unconditionally reconciling with a person when boundaries still need to be firmly established.

Rather, forgiveness comes from the Person and work of Christ the forgiver. He wants to do His forgiving work in and through us. It is a heart matter, and it must include the mind, will, and emotions in order to be complete. Forgiveness releases the person doing the forgiving, freeing them from the poison of toxic emotions. It releases perpetrators so that God can work in their lives, cancelling the debt held against the other person.

When we practice a lifestyle of forgiveness, we cease to sit in the place of judgment, releasing all offenses done against us. And furthermore, forgiveness is commanded by the Word of God—it is not optional or only a good suggestion. Again, let's take a few minutes to meditate on these principles, asking God to apply them to our life through His Spirit.

Real World, Practical Forgiveness

We would be surprised to learn how many Christians—that's right, *Christians*—are offended at the suggestion that they might need to forgive someone. "I've already done that!" they adamantly claim. However, their forgiveness has never yet dealt with their emotions or the deep issues of their heart.

Most Christians sincerely want to get the forgiveness thing right. Their religious pride is hurt if we suggest they still may be trapped in a prison of anger and unforgiveness. In many cases, they probably just need a better explanation of forgiveness, what it means, and how it applies to their lives.

Many believers don't understand how practical forgiveness is for everyday life. We don't have to wonder whether or not we've truly forgiven someone who has wronged us, for there are tell-tale symptoms that our unforgiveness remains. Do we still feel hurt inside because of what someone did to us in the past? Are we still angry when we talk about some injustice that was done to us? Do we still cringe when we think of someone—perhaps a family member, coworker, church member, or pastor? Do we find ourselves going out of our way to avoid a particular person even though they've asked for our forgiveness and we have no reason to fear them?

If we answered yes to one or more of the above questions, it doesn't mean we haven't tried to forgive the other person; it just means our emotions have not yet been impacted. Only then can we truly be emotionally free. We need to experience complete forgiveness, not just *trying* to forgive by our own willpower. Forgiveness is a supernatural experience, exchanging negative emotions for God's peace. It is the only thing that will deal with our emotions and bring relief once and for all.

A husband and wife scheduled a prayer appointment with us a few years ago. They came in and sat down on the sofa, and we asked them to close their eyes and pray. When we asked the wife to tell us where she needed to apply forgiveness, she smiled and said, "Oh, I have forgiven *everyone* in my whole life!" And yes, she stressed the "everyone."

Immediately, her husband looked at her in astonishment and said, "Well, what about your sister Eleanor and our neighbor Karl? And what about your anger toward our son Andy for not coming home for Thanksgiving? And don't forget about being mad at your mother for always criticizing your cooking and..." on and on he went.

Stories like this are more common than one might imagine. Many people are simply out of touch with their emotions and what's really going on in their heart. Psychologists like to call it denial, and that's part of it. However, it's also a self-induced numbness that causes us to tune out our unpleasant emotions. That doesn't mean they've gone away, it only means we've simply stuffed them deep into subconscious memory where they are buried alive.

If we feel an unpleasant emotion when we think of any person or situation, then we still need some real-world, hands-on forgiveness. The truth is that none of us have fully dealt with every single unresolved hurt, offense, or fear we've encountered in our entire lifetime. We would have to be perfect in order to accomplish that feat. And if we actually believe we are perfect, then we have an even *bigger* problem than we realize—and we need forgiveness for trying to be God.

Forgiveness Isn't Difficult

Forgiveness doesn't need to be complicated or difficult. Yet Dennis and I have made a startling discovery as we've ministered in numerous churches and Bible schools, with hundreds of prayer appointments with individuals seeking relief from their inner pain. Shocking as it may sound, we have noticed that between

90–99 percent of the Christians we minister to have no idea how to forgive effectively enough to deal with their negative emotions.

Occasionally, someone will forgive another person "accidentally," even though they don't know what they did or how they did it. One example of this is that of Corrie Ten Boom. During the Nazi occupation of Holland in World War II, Corrie and her sister, Betsie, were sent to Ravensbruck concentration camp after they were caught hiding Jews in their home.

After the war ended, Corrie was giving her testimony in a church in Munich. Following her stirring message about the forgiveness of God, a man made his way through the crowd to speak to her. She was aghast when she realized he had been one of the guards at Ravensbruck, but he did not recognize Corrie as a former inmate. He told her he had been a guard at a concentration camp during the war, but had since been forgiven by God. Now he was a fellow Christian.

Smiling broadly, he stretched out his hand to shake Corrie's. She writes of that time:

> And I, who had spoken so glibly of forgiveness, fumbled in my pocketbook rather than take that hand. He would not remember me, of course—how could he remember one prisoner among those thousands of women?
>
> But I remembered him and the leather crop swinging from his belt. I was face to face with one of my captors and my blood seemed to freeze.... It could not have been many seconds that he stood there—hand held out—but to me it seemed hours as I wrestled with the most difficult thing I had ever had to do.
>
> For I had to do it—I knew that...

And still I stood there with the coldness clutching my heart. But forgiveness is not an emotion—I knew that too. Forgiveness is an act of the will, and the will can function regardless of the temperature of the heart. "Help!" I prayed silently. "I can lift my hand. I can do that much. You supply the feeling."

And so woodenly, mechanically, I thrust my hand into the one stretched out to me. And as I did, an incredible thing took place. The current started in my shoulder, raced down my arm, sprang into our joined hands. And then this healing warmth seemed to flood my whole being, bringing tears to my eyes.

"I forgive you, brother!" I cried. "With all my heart!"[1]

I wonder how many people have tried to forgive by shaking hands after reading Corrie's story. It wasn't the shaking of hands that released forgiveness, but the God encounter that accomplished the forgiveness. As she obediently reached her hand out to the guard, she forgave by the grace of Christ the forgiver in her heart.

A man named Charlie told us that he had forgiven when he pretended a pillow was the neck of a perpetrator. He strangled the pillow, then somehow the anger left as he let go. Charlie accidentally forgave in his heart as he let go with his hands. We explained to Charlie that forgiveness didn't take place in his hands, but it was his heart that cooperated with Christ the forgiver.

Much quality ministry has happened to us at times even though we didn't understand how it happened or how to make it happen again. If we don't know how to do something properly, we may just keep doing the wrong thing repeatedly while hoping it might work. Occasionally the heart cooperates with the words or actions, but forgiveness is not in shaking hands, letting go of an object, or praying long enough or hard enough. That is why some have adopted the theory that forgiveness is a process, and often a lifelong one at that. Many have genuinely tried to forgive but they have tried the wrong way. But when properly understood, forgiveness is easy.

ENDNOTE

1.   Corrie Ten Boom, *The Hiding Place* (Old Tappan, NJ: Chosen Books, Fleming H. Revel Co., 1971), 215.

Chapter 11

EASY DOES IT

By Dr. Jen

Forgiveness Really Is Easy

A few years ago, we invited a young French woman to stay with us for several weeks. She had lived in France her whole life and had never visited America before. When we arrived home from the airport, we showed her where everything was in the rooms where she would be staying. Then we spent a short time talking and said our good-nights.

In the morning, we were dismayed to discover she had been awake until 2 A.M. trying to figure out how to turn off the lamps in the bedroom. Finally, she gave up and just unplugged the lamps so she could get some sleep. Apparently, American lamps have different switches than French lamps! We then showed her how to turn the switches on and off. It was easy when she knew how to do it.

Forgiveness is the same way. When we know how to do it the right way, it's easy. We've seen people, who have struggled with this for years, "turn the forgiveness switch" in mere moments after they learned the secret.

Forgiveness Sets Us Free

Jesus said that bitterness and resentment are like jailers that keep us imprisoned (see Matt. 18:21-35). The person who did us wrong may be living a happy, carefree life, but our own feelings take us captive. We replay the situation repeatedly in our head, and we feel a churning in our gut every time we think about them. What we may not know is that even the cells of our body are being poisoned by our anger. It's like us gulping down a vile cup of poison while saying smugly, "I'll show them!"

The following story from the San Diego news is a dramatic testimony of forgiveness in the face of horrendous circumstances:

> Molly LaRue's body was found next to her dead fiancé. They were murdered by serial killer Paul David Crews in September 1990 while hiking on the Appalachian Trail.
>
> Sixteen years later, just before Christmas, Molly's father, Jim LaRue, was in a Pennsylvania courtroom reading a one-page letter of forgiveness to Crews when his death sentence was commuted to life in prison without parole.
>
> "Most people think you are forgiving the perpetrator and they're off scot-free and you get nothing," says LaRue, who lives in a suburb near Cleveland. "It's just the opposite. When you forgive a person, you're deciding to be freed."

He has no doubt that forgiveness has been good for him. "I have the energy to focus on other things," he says. Before, "there were always nagging, gnawing thoughts in the background. You pay a price for that."[1]

Forgiveness washes away buried pain and brings healing for even the deepest emotional traumas. It replaces toxic emotions with the peace of God. But we don't have to reserve it for times of enormous injury. Forgiveness is also freely available to cleanse every bit of guilt, embarrassment, anger, bitterness, anxiety, fear, hate, and grief—whether large or small.

Forgiveness has internal cleansing power. We experience this cleansing for the first time at conversion, when the sin barriers that separated us from God are washed away. When we opened our heart, experienced forgiveness and cleansing, we were no longer separated from God (see 1 John 1:9). With the barriers removed, we instantly experienced peace.

But forgiveness is not meant to be a one-time, or a just-when-I-really-need-it gift that we keep on the shelf the rest of the time. Jesus also gave us the gift of forgiveness for our everyday use. We can hang it by the bed as we sleep at night and take hold of it when our feet hit the floor in the morning. It is meant for our lifestyle, walking it day in and day out.

Unforgiveness Makes Us Sick

Medical doctors and researchers have found clear evidence that physical health is closely connected to our emotional health. For a long time, researchers have realized that emotional baggage often leads to disease. Some researchers even make a distinction between stress and emotions. But stress is fear based, so it is emotional too.[2]

Since the 1990s, scientific research has been exploding on the subject of forgiveness. Research indicates a strong correlation between unforgiveness and sickness.[3] Medical doctors and researchers are turning to forgiveness as one of the primary keys for dealing with toxic emotions.

This is quite a dramatic reversal of scientific opinion. Scientists and medical doctors used to scoff at the idea that "unquantifiable emotions" could be given any consideration in serious medicine. However, the results of extensive research cannot be denied.

The molecules of emotion, which are called neuropeptides, directly influence every organ at the cellular level. In time, our emotions are written into our cellular memory. Over a lifetime, our biography becomes our biology. Our brain is in constant dialogue with our gut and our entire body through the emotions. Our mind and body are not just connected—they are unified in one system. This mind-body unity is now undisputed by researchers.

Although negative emotions don't directly cause disease, they create the conditions by which diseases can develop. There is actually a new field of medicine called psychoneuroimmunology, or psychoneuroimmunoendocrinology, which treats the toxic interactions between emotions and physiology.

Emotions and Physical Health

Although there is merit in our culture's current emphasis on exercise and nutrition, it doesn't matter much what else we do if we are poisoning our body with negative emotions. It should come as no surprise to learn that Dennis and I see many physical healings occur when a person forgives. Here are just a few samples:

- Janine, from North Carolina, wrote, "First, I got healed of rejection from my mother. After that,

I was amazed to see a skin cancer on my arm get smaller and smaller over the next few weeks, until it totally disappeared. My doctor was simply astounded. I didn't have to have surgery! It was just gone!"

- And Ronda, from Mt. Pleasant, South Carolina, wrote to us some time ago, saying, "I was so twisted up with arthritis that I could barely use my hands. I could hardly bear the pain at times. But when I prayed with the Clarks and received emotional healing, my arthritis went away too. My fingers have straightened out and, praise God, there's no more pain!"

Anger and hostility may even lead to an early death. A long-term study showed that people who score in the high range on hostility scales are almost five times more likely to die of heart disease than those scoring lower. Furthermore, they were seven times more likely to die by age 50.[4]

Chronic pain has also been linked to toxic emotions. Dr. John Sarno, professor of rehabilitative medicine in New York University School of Medicine, found that 88 percent of his patients had a wide range of negative emotional issues that were physically affecting them. When he treated the underlying emotions, he observed that his patients rapidly improved, and many were permanently cured.[5]

Stress, Aging, and Fear

Stress is a combination of emotional distress and physical tension. It arises from a fear-based negative perception of one's ability to control the circumstances of life. Toxic emotions can lead to stress even when our circumstances don't warrant it. Buried emotions cause internal pressure. The exertion of willpower, which is necessary for emotional suppression, generates stress regardless of our external situation. In other words, we can actually create our own stress.

The emotional toll of chronic stress accelerates the normal aging process in the body. A study published by Elissa Eppel in 2004 documents how chronic stress speeds up the aging process on the cellular level. Stress alters the immune system and our ability to produce blood cells. It is also associated with physical frailty, osteoporosis, inflammatory arthritis, cardiovascular disease, and general functional decline.[6]

About 40 million American adults 18 years and older suffer from anxiety disorders. That is approximately 18 percent of the population in a given year.[7] Anxiety disorders are the most common form of mental illness in the United States, which include panic disorder, obsessive-compulsive disorder (OCD), post-traumatic stress injury (PTSI), generalized anxiety disorder (GAD), and phobias (social phobia, agoraphobia, and specific phobia).[8]

Many diseases have been linked with fear and anxiety,[9] including skin disorders such as eczema and psoriasis, high blood pressure, cardiovascular diseases, and digestive conditions such as ulcers, colitis, irritable bowel syndrome (IBS), and Crohn's disease.

A month or two after Dennis and I were married in 1997, I was jerked awake out of a sound sleep by a rapidly racing and pounding heartbeat and a cold sweat. I knew exactly what was happening: paroxysmal atrial tachycardia (PAT). This consists of extremely rapid heartbeats for a period that begins and ends abruptly. The heart rate suddenly shoots upward to 140–220 beats a minute, and it feels like it simply won't slow down.

My heart was beating so fast that it felt like the bed was shaking. This was not a new thing, but a symptom that had tormented me several times a month for the past 20 years. Dennis awakened and felt my fear flooding the room, while I felt fear mainly in my gut but also surrounding me. Fortunately, he helped me pray through this. I received forgiveness and instantly the fear was replaced by peace, and the fear in the room left. My heart immediately stopped palpitating and returned to a gentle, normal rhythm. The atrial tachycardia never recurred again.

It is important for us to remember that heart health—like so many other aspects of our physical body—is linked to toxic emotions, including fear, stress, depression, and anger.[10]

Shame, Depression, and Repressed Emotions

Guilt and shame are often associated with depression. Guilt arises from a sense of having done something wrong, while shame usually arises from a perception of personal unworthiness, embarrassment, disgrace, or dishonor.

A person suffering from guilt or shame typically reflects it in their body language, such as lowering their gaze to avoid eye contact, hanging their head down low, or walking with drooping shoulders. Often, such a person feels helpless and hopeless, and these feelings can lead to social isolation and depression, which has been linked to heart disease,[11] osteoporosis,[12] and cancer.[13]

It's important to understand that we can't find deep relief from our emotional pain by merely suppressing our negative emotions. Suppressed negative emotions don't actually go away, they're just hidden away under the surface of our conscious awareness.[14] Emotions don't die; we just "bury them alive."

Suppressed emotions function much like termites, secretly eating away at the wooden structure of a house. Although the homeowner might not even realize termites are there, the destruction continues nonetheless. In the same way, the suppression of negative emotions can adversely affect the cardiovascular system.[15] Emotional suppression is also associated with an increase in coronary heart disease[16] and cancer.[17]

Consider the words of Gabor Maté, MD, a Vancouver physician and the author of *When the Body Says No: The Cost of Hidden Stress*.[18] Here is an excerpt from an article Dr. Maté wrote:

> "I never get angry," says a character in one of Woody Allen's movies, "I grow a tumor instead." In over two decades of family medicine, including seven years of palliative care work, I have been struck by how consistently the lives of people with chronic illness are characterized by emotional shutdown: the paralysis of "negative" emotions—in particular, anger.
>
> This pattern holds true in a wide range of diseases from cancer, rheumatoid arthritis and multiple sclerosis to inflammatory bowel disorder, chronic fatigue syndrome, and amyotrophic lateral sclerosis (ALS)...
>
> The suppression of anger contributes to the onset of cancer and other diseases because the mind and body cannot be separated. The brain's emotional center is directly and powerfully linked with the body's immune system. Emotions such as anger serve exactly the same defensive role as the immune system: to protect our boundaries and to keep us from being overwhelmed by external forces. Similarly, both emotions and the immune system, when

healthy, also serve a repair function: they help us to heal when we have sustained some trauma or when something has gone wrong internally.[19]

The Science of Forgiveness

Scientific research on forgiveness has exploded since the 1990s, and hundreds of studies by researchers in many fields are focusing on everything from the emotional, mental, and physical benefits of forgiveness to the relational and societal implications. The social sciences have linked forgiveness to social bonding in communities, overcoming the effects of violent crimes, improved physical health, and having successful marriages.

Forgiveness is good for our heart—literally. A study in the *Journal of Behavioral Medicine* links forgiveness with lower blood pressure and also with stress relief.[20] Another study correlates forgiveness with needing less medication and experiencing better quality of sleep, less fatigue, alleviation of various physical symptoms, and an improvement in overall physical health.[21]

An article published in the January 2008 issue of the Mayo Clinic *Women's HealthSource* states,

> Holding a grudge appears to affect the cardiovascular and nervous systems. In one study, people who focused on a personal grudge had elevated blood pressure and heart rates, as well as increased muscle tension and feelings of being less in control. When asked to imagine forgiving the person who had hurt them, the participants said they felt more positive and relaxed and thus, the changes dissipated. Other studies have shown that forgiveness has beneficial effects on psychological health, too.[22]

Dennis and I regularly see people experience dramatic physical healings as a result of forgiving others. A young mother had been diagnosed with four serious medical conditions. A friend gave her our materials, which explained how forgiveness and the God-tools for emotional health also impact physical healing. When she prayed through her painful memories and toxic emotions, her symptoms disappeared. A new round of medical tests verified that she was completely healed.

The Gift of Forgiveness

We should pay very close attention to someone's dying words. In the final days before Angela's husband died, he tried to tell her all the important things she would need to know after his passing. She strained to hear every word and wrote down everything he said. The dying husband told Angela how much he loved her, of course. But he also told her details about important practical matters, such as which people she could trust with financial matters, what to do, and what to avoid. She kept a meticulous record of all these things. Everything he told her proved to be crucial for the future life she led. She was extremely grateful for his love and guidance.

And in much the same way, Jesus chose His final words carefully before He died on the cross. Forgiveness was so important for our redemption that Jesus declared it through His final prayer for humankind and His final action on behalf of one man. First, He prayed, *"Father, forgive them"* (Luke 23:34). Then He forgave a criminal hanging on the cross beside Him: *"Assuredly, I say to you, today you will be with Me in Paradise"* (Luke 23:43).

Jesus died to give us this wonderful gift of forgiveness. All Christians recognize that this gift of forgiveness is the key to their initial salvation and right standing with God. There is no substitute for forgiveness. It is the indispens-able gateway to God's kingdom. However, as vital as forgiveness is for our initial entrance into the Christian life, it is so much more than that. Forgiveness is also our key to the elusive "abundant life" Christians talk about but too rarely experience.

A Process or Instantaneous?

When we first received Christ, we opened our heart to Him, received forgiveness, and instantly experienced peace. This was wonderful, but Paul goes on to say we should continue to walk in Christ in the same way we received Him: *"As you have therefore received Christ...[so] walk (regulate your lives and conduct your-selves) in union with and conformity to Him"* (Col. 2:6 AMP). The word *walk* refers to the way we live everyday life. This is the way to make forgiveness a lifestyle instead of a one-time event.

Many experts have taught that forgiveness is a *process* that may take a long time to go through. But think about this: Was our initial conversion a process, or was it instantaneous? As soon as we asked Jesus to come into our heart, He was there for us. When we first received forgiveness from Him, did we have to fast, plead, or experience a long delay? Of course not. When we got saved, we didn't have to work for forgiveness or beg God for it; we just received it by opening the door of our heart in faith.

Forgiveness is not just a choice. It is a gift. Because of what Jesus did for us on the cross, forgiveness is freely available and eas-ily accessible. It is the way to live life well. Forgiveness begins with a choice but it ends with an encounter with Christ the forgiver.

Experiencing Christ the Forgiver

Before I met Dennis, I tried and tried to forgive. To my sur-prise, he told me that had been the whole problem: *I* was trying to do it. He pointed out that it's by grace through faith that we are saved (see Eph. 2:8-9). Grace is the personal presence of Christ empowering us to be all that He has called us to be and do all that He has called us to do.

The apostle Paul wrote, *"It is no longer I who live, but Christ who lives in me"* (Gal. 2:20), which suggests that it is also no longer I who loves, nor I who forgives. Christ is He who forgives through me; it is He who loves through me. You and I do not extend forgiveness by ourselves, from ourselves. Forgiveness is a Person, an encounter with Someone, a supernatural exchange that takes place.

Christ the forgiver living inside us does all the work. True forgiveness requires encountering Christ the forgiver rather than knowing and reciting Scripture verses, or merely understanding a doctrine of forgiveness. It is no longer I who loves, but Christ who loves in and through me. It is no longer I who forgives, but Christ the forgiver who forgives through me. And that's not just true of the mighty apostle; it's true of every believer. It is the power of Christ Himself in us and working through us; or as Paul says, *"Christ in you, the hope of glory"* (Col. 1:27).

So why do so many believers live in defeat and despair? Since Christ lives in them, the potential for victory is certainly there, but somehow they're failing to cooperate with that potential and appropriate the power. Paul didn't just see this in some kind of abstract theoretical or theological way. No, it was a reality for him. He actually allowed Christ to live through him, and he realized that was the secret of the Christian life.

Unfortunately, it's entirely possible to go on living as we lived before after we are born again, living in the power of our own flesh and intellect. Rather than letting Jesus live His life through us, we can live a life of striving and struggle as we try to please God.

If you're like most of us, you've experienced this yourself. There have been times when you tried to live the Christian life in your own strength, or you tried to forgive someone in your own power. Paul, in Romans 7, described his own miserable experience with this misguided approach to the Christian life: *"O wretched man that I am! Who will deliver me from this body of death?"* (Rom. 7:24).

So what is the answer to this question? Let's take a look at a story from the life of Jesus. Jesus went to Capernaum, and people heard He was in a house. So many had gathered together that there was no more room for anyone else to come. As He was preaching to them, some men brought their paralyzed friend to the meeting to be healed. But because the house was too crowded, they lowered him through the roof so Jesus couldn't miss him. And instead of physically healing the man right here, Jesus said,

> *"Son, your sins are forgiven you."*
>
> *And some of the scribes were sitting there and reasoning in their hearts, "Why does this Man speak blasphemies like this? Who can forgive sins but God alone?"*
>
> *But immediately, when Jesus perceived in His spirit that they reasoned thus within themselves, He said to them, "Why do you reason about these things in your hearts? Which is easier, to say to the paralytic, 'Your sins are forgiven you,' or to say, 'Arise, take up your bed and walk'? But that you may know that the Son of Man has power on earth to forgive sins"—He said to the paralytic, "I say to you, arise, take up your bed, and go to your house." Immediately he arose, took up*

the bed, and went out in the presence of them all,
so that all were amazed and glorified God, saying,
"We never saw anything like this!" (Mark 2:5-12)

The scribes were upset that Jesus told the paralytic that his sins were forgiven. Why? They reasoned correctly that only God can forgive sins. So by saying this, Jesus was making Himself the equivalent of God. Then He told them it was just as easy for Him to forgive sins as it was to physically heal a man who was paralyzed. Easy. Instantaneous.

We make forgiveness hard when we try to do what only God can do. So what is the answer? Let the One who forgives sins do it. We somehow managed to cooperate with Him when we were born again. Was it hard? Not at all. We simply yielded our heart to Him and received forgiveness from Christ the forgiver.

So remember Paul's words in Colossians 2:6 (NIV): *"Just as you received Christ Jesus as Lord, continue to live in Him."* Forgiveness isn't hard or complicated. Easy does it!

ENDNOTES

1. S. Dolbee, "The healing power of forgiveness: Science measures physical as well as mental benefits," *San Diego Times Tribune,* August 16, 2008.

2. W. Cannon, "The role of emotion in disease," *Annals of Internal Medicine*, Philadelphia, 9, (1936), 453-1465.

3. E. L. Worthington Jr., J. W. Berry, and L. Parrott III, "Unforgiveness, forgiveness, religion, and health." Quoted in T. G. Plante and A. C. Sherman (Eds.), *Faith and health: Psychological Perspectives*, (New York: Guilford Press, 2001), 107-138.

4. J. C. Barefoot, G. Dahlstrom, and R. B. Williams, "Hostility, CHD incidence, and total mortality: a 25-year follow-up study of 255 physicians," *Psychosomatic Medicine*, 45, (1983), 59-63.

5. J. Sarno, *The Mindbody Prescription: Healing the Body, Healing the Pain* (New York: Warner Books, 1999), xviii-xxviii.

6. E. S. Epel, E. H. Blackburn, J. Lin, F. S. Dhabhar, N. E. Adler, J. D. Morrow, and R. M. Cawthon, "Accelerated telomere shortening in response to life stress," *Proceedings of the National Academies of Science*, 101(49), (2004), 17312-17315.

7. U.S. Census Bureau Population Estimates by Demographic Characteristics. Table 2: Annual Estimates of the Population by Selected Age Groups and Sex for the United States: April 1, 2000 to July 1, 2004 (NC-EST2004-02) Source: Population Division, U.S. Census Bureau, Release Date: June 9, 2005.

8.   R. Kessler, P. Berglund, O. Demler, R. Jin, and E. Walters, "Lifetime prevalence and age-of-onset distributions of DSM-IV disorders in the National Comorbidity Survey Replication (NCS-R)," *Archives of General Psychiatry*, 62(6), (2005), 593-602. R. Kessler, W. Chiu, O. Demler, and E. Walters, "Prevalence, severity, and comorbidity of twelve-month DSM-IV disorders in the National Comorbidity Survey Replication (NCS-R)" *Archives of General Psychiatry*, 62(6), (2005), 617-27. R. Kessler, P. Berglund, O. Demler, R. Jin, and E. Walters, "Lifetime prevalence and age-of-onset distributions of DSM-IV disorders in the National Comorbidity Survey Replication (NCS-R)" *Archives of General Psychiatry*, 62(6), (2005), 593-602.

9.   S. Cohen, D. Janicki-Devert, and G. E. Miller, "Psychological Stress and Disease," *Journal of the American Medical Association*, 298(14), (2007), 1685-1687.

10.   D. Brotman, S. Golden, I. Wittstein, "The cardiovascular toll of stress," *Lancet*, 2007 Dec 1; 370(9602), 1828. L. Kubzansky, and R. Thurston, "Emotional vitality and incident coronary heart disease: Benefits of healthy psychological functioning," *Archives of General Psychiatry*, 2007, Dec; 64, 1393.

11.   T. Rutledge, S. E. Reis, M. Olson, et al., "Psychosocial Variables Are Associated with Atherosclerosis Risk Factors Among Women with Chest Pain: the WISE [Women's Ischemia Syndrome Evaluation] Study," *Psychosomatic Medicine*, 6, (2001), 282-288.

12.   R. Yirmiyah, and I. Bab, "Major Depression Is a Risk Factor for Low Bone Mineral Density: A Meta-Analysis," *Biological Psychiatry*, Volume 66, Issue 5, September 1, 2009, 423-432.

13. L. Pyter, V. Pineros, J. Galang, M. McClintock, and B. Prendergast, "Peripheral tumors induce depressive-like behaviors and cytokine production and alter hypothalamic-pituitary-adrenal axis regulation," *Proceedings of the National Academy of Sciences*, 106 (22), (2008), 9069-9074.

14. J. Gross, "The emerging field of emotion regulation: An integrative review," *Review of General Psychology*, 2, (1998), 271-299.

15. J. Gross, and R. Levenson, "Hiding feelings: The acute effects of inhibiting positive and negative emotions," *Journal of Abnormal Psychology*, 106, (1997), 95-103.

16. J. Pennebaker, "Inhibition as the linchpin of health" Quoted in H. S. Friedman (Ed.), "Hostility, coping, and health," Washington, DC: American Psychological Association, (1992), 127-139.

17. J. Gross, "Emotional expression in cancer onset and progression," *Social Science in Medicine*, 28, (1989), 1239-1248. M. Jensen, "Psychobiological factors predicting the course of breast cancer," *Journal of Personality*, 55, (1987), 317-342. L. Temoshok, "Personality, coping style, emotion, and cancer: Towards an integrative model," *Cancer Surveys*, 6, (1987), 545-567.

18. G. Maté, *When the Body Says No: The Cost of Hidden Stress* (Canada: Knopf, 2003).

19. G. Maté, "Suppressing Our Emotions Harms Physical and Mental Health," (April 2004). Retrieved January 13, 2010, from Alive.com: http://www.alive.com/1787a5a2 .php?subject_bread_cramb=78.

20. K. Lawler, J. Younger, R. Piferi, E. Billington, R. Jobe, K. Edmondson, and W. H. Jones, "A change of heart: cardiovascular correlates of forgiveness in response to interpersonal conflict," *Journal of Behavioral Medicine*, 26, (2003), 373-393.

21. K. Lawler, J. Younger, R. Piferi, R. Jobe, K. Edmondson, and W. Jones, "The unique effects of forgiveness on health: an exploration of pathways," *Journal of Behavioral Medicine*, 28, (2005), 157-167.

22. Mayo Clinic, "Learning to Forgive May Improve Well-Being," (Wednesday, January 2, 2008), Mayo Clinic Women's HealthSource. Retrieved October 12, 2010, from the Mayo Clinic website: http://www.mayoclinic.org/news2008-mchi/4405.html.

Chapter 12

THE GOD-TOOLS

By Dr. Jen

The Victorious Christian Life

Scripture tells us that we've already received all of the spiritual equipment we need to live a victorious Christian life. In fact, Paul calls this spiritual equipment "God-tools," which God has given to us for deep emotional healing. But few believers seem to know how to use them properly. Paul writes:

> *We use our powerful God-tools for smashing warped philosophies, tearing down barriers erected against the truth of God, fitting every loose thought and emotion and impulse into the structure of life shaped by Christ* (2 Corinthians 10:5 MSG).

And again:

> *God is strong, and He wants you strong. So take everything the Master has set out for you, well-made*

weapons of the best materials. And put them to use
(Ephesians 6:10-11 MSG).

Reality television shows are popular these days, but the Christian experience should be the greatest reality makeover show of all time. Have you ever tried to keep New Year's resolutions? Or change a destructive habit? Or stop thinking certain thoughts?

The Bible talks frequently about transformation, but many Christians don't seem to actually experience much transformation other than their initial salvation experience. What's the problem here? Paul explains: *"That you put off...the old man...and that you put on the new man which was created according to God, in true righteousness and holiness"* (Eph. 4:22-24).

There is a process in-between "putting off the old" and "putting on the new." How do we put off the old and how do we put on the new man that is created according to God in righteousness and holiness? If we don't understand how to do that process, there is going to be little change in our lives over the long run. But if we can get this right, then transformation will happen quickly, bringing along with it emotional healing.

In all my years of church experience before I met Dennis, I honestly couldn't detect much transformation in the lives of believers in my church or through Christian counseling ministries. In fact, I was getting very discouraged about the lack of spiritual progress I saw in most people, including myself.

I remember a time when my church was planning an evangelistic crusade. But as I looked around at the church members, I couldn't help but think, "Maybe we should first do something to bring healing and victory to the believers we already have, before trying to make more converts like them!" It was so sad. Our church was filled with well-meaning Christians who were stressed out, wounded, grouchy, fearful, and depressed. "What is wrong here? Shouldn't Christians be in better shape than this?" I asked myself.

Something that Works

I don't know about you, but I simply don't have time for theories or practices that don't work. None of us have time or energy to go on rabbit trails that only become dead ends. We want biblical tools that bring true transformation into the daily fabric of our lives.

Well, the good news is that the God-tools really work, and they can be easily applied to our life. I've been thrilled to discover both physiological and spiritual principles for transformation. And through Dennis's mentoring, I've learned why the God-tools work so well, and I've learned how to use them effectively.

This is not a method, but a descriptive explanation that demystifies how to live in the Spirit of God. If God is always present to save, then He is always present to sanctify. From the initial encounter with Christ to the subsequent relationship that follows, we have documented a step-by-step practical explanation that combines God encounters with process.

Let's take another look at Romans 12:2:

> *And do not be conformed to this world, but be transformed by the renewing of your mind, that you may prove what is that good and acceptable and perfect will of God.*

The Greek word Paul uses for "mind" (*nous*) doesn't mean just our thoughts or what is going on in our heads. *Nous* means our entire being, which includes our thoughts, will, emotions, reflective consciousness, perception, and understanding. Our mind encompasses our whole heart (including our emotions), not just our thinking faculties.

The ramifications of this are huge. If a person truly wants to be transformed, something has to be done about their pesky emotions, not just their thoughts or intellectual questions. Of course, some people assume it's impossible to do much to change our emotions. But they are so wrong. Our emotions—and the rest of our mind as well—can be transformed through basic, essential God-tools every believer has already been given by the Lord. We've already received all the spiritual equipment we need to live a godly life.

God-Tool #1: Prayer

Prayer is the first God-tool that we've been given in Christ. The four main components of simple prayer, once again, are honoring God as a Person, listening to God (listening is awareness that includes the spiritual "inner knowings" of seeing, hearing, and touching), time spent with God, and function and flow. The first three elements have been covered previously, but now let's focus on the fourth element: function and flow.

Jesus lived His life on earth in the function and flow of the Spirit of God. The early church followed Christ's example, cooperating with the moving of the Holy Spirit through loving intercession, releasing, receiving, and forgiving. Let's look at some specific examples of this.

Jesus was in constant communion with Father God, following His guidance as to what He was to do and say at any given time (see John 5:19). This spiritual communion with the Father was of utmost importance to Jesus. He said:

> *I do nothing of Myself; but as My Father taught Me,*
> *I speak these things. And He who sent Me is with*

*Me. The Father has not left Me alone, for I always
do those things that please Him* (John 8:28-29).

Jesus also told His disciples, *"My food is to do the will of Him
who sent Me, and to finish His work"* (John 4:34).

When Jesus ministered to others, He was aware of the "spiritual flow" that took place in His body. When the woman with
a hemorrhage was healed by touching the hem of His garment,
Jesus explained, *"Someone did touch Me; for I perceived that [heal-
ing] power has gone forth from Me"* (Luke 8:46 AMP).

He encouraged His disciples that they could count on the
Father to be with them too, giving them the right words to speak
in every situation:

> *When they deliver you up, do not worry about how
> or what you should speak. For it will be given to you
> in that hour what you should speak; for it is not you
> who speak, but the Spirit of your Father who speaks
> in you* (Matthew 10:19-20).

The apostle John reminded his readers that he had experienced
an incredibly close relationship with Jesus during His earthly ministry: *"That which was from the beginning, which we have heard, which
we have seen with our eyes, which we have looked upon, and our hands
have handled, concerning the Word of life"* (1 John 1:1). But the story
doesn't stop there. John went on to say that he was still experiencing
Jesus's reality many years after He had already ascended back to the
Father. And he said this same kind of relationship with the Lord
was available to every other Christian as well:

> *The life was manifested, and we have seen, and bear
> witness, and declare to you that eternal life which
> was with the Father and was manifested to us—that*

> *which we have seen and heard we declare to you,*
> *that you also may have fellowship with us; and truly*
> *our fellowship is with the Father and with His Son*
> *Jesus Christ. And these things we write to you that*
> *your joy may be full* (1 John 1:2-4).

How would you like your peace and joy to "be full"? It comes through having intimate, unhindered fellowship with Christ. That can be your experience today.

The Many Facets of Prayer

Like a beautiful diamond, prayer is a wondrous, many-faceted relationship with God. This includes loving intercession, releasing, receiving, forgiving, and resisting. Each of these facets is critical for experiencing and imparting the deep relief available in the presence of the Lord.

Loving Intercession

Jesus bridged the gap between heaven and earth. His intercession on behalf of humanity released heavenly power into the earthly realm. And He taught us to pray He would manifest more of the reality of His kingdom *"on earth as it is in heaven"* (Matt. 6:10). Through our loving intercession, we can release heavenly rivers on earth. Jesus said:

> *Whoever drinks of the water that I shall give him*
> *will never thirst. But the water that I shall give him*
> *will become in him a fountain of water springing up*
> *into everlasting life* (John 4:14).

> *He that believeth on Me, as the scripture hath said,*
> *out of his belly shall flow rivers of living water* (John
> 7:38 KJV).

There is tangible spiritual substance in the prayers of believers. In the Book of Revelation, we're told that the prayers we release from our spirit are actually stored in heaven until it's time for them to be poured out and answered on the earth: *"Now when He had taken the scroll, the four living creatures and the twenty-four elders fell down before the Lamb, each having a harp, and golden bowls full of incense, which are the prayers of the saints"* (Rev. 5:8; see also 8:3-5).

Practice: Close your eyes and "drop down." From your heart, yield to Christ within and allow loving intercession to flow out to your loved ones or friends. That is true intercession, "loving even without words."

Releasing (Letting Go)

Jesus said He came to the earth to do the will of Father God rather than fulfill His own will. This means He released, or let go of, His own preferences and choices: *"He knelt down and prayed, saying, 'Father, if it is Your will, take this cup away from Me; nevertheless not My will, but Yours, be done'"* (Luke 22:41-42).

In the same way, believers are called to be obedient to God's will, making Jesus the Lord of their lives. This is not optional but mandatory if we are to live a victorious Christian life. Jesus once asked, *"Why do you call Me 'Lord, Lord,' and not do the things which I say?"* (Luke 6:46). Making Him Lord means yielding, releasing, letting go, and obeying what He tells us to do.

Practice: Close your eyes in prayer and "drop down," focusing on Christ in your heart. Can you picture any area of your life that causes you to feel tense? From your belly, yield and release it to God. As you release, let it go from your heart—not just mentally. Notice that you feel deep peace when you actually do release your painful or stressful areas to the Lord.

Receiving

Jesus received a powerful spiritual baptism from His Father. Luke records:

> *Jesus also was baptized; and while He prayed, the heaven was opened. And the Holy Spirit descended in bodily form like a dove upon Him, and a voice came from heaven which said, "You are My beloved Son; in You I am well pleased"* (Luke 3:21-22).

On several occasions, the believers in the Book of Acts received a similar spiritual impartation:

> *When the Day of Pentecost had fully come, they were all with one accord in one place. And suddenly there came a sound from heaven, as of a rushing mighty wind, and it filled the whole house where they were sitting. Then there appeared to them divided tongues, as of fire, and one sat upon each of them. And they were all filled with the Holy Spirit...* (Acts 2:1-4).

> *When they had prayed, the place where they were assembled together was shaken; and they were all filled with the Holy Spirit, and they spoke the word of God with boldness* (Acts 4:31).

This matter of "receiving" is found throughout the New Testament. In the Book of Ephesians, Paul prays for believers to receive inner revelation and strengthening:

> *Therefore I also, after I heard of your faith in the Lord Jesus and your love for all the saints, do not cease to give thanks for you, making mention of you in my prayers: that the God of our Lord Jesus Christ, the Father of glory, may give to you the spirit of wisdom and revelation in the knowledge of Him, the eyes of your understanding being enlightened; that you may know what is the hope of His calling, what are the riches of the glory of His inheritance in the saints, and what is the exceeding greatness of His power toward us who believe, according to the working of His mighty power which He worked in Christ when He raised Him from the dead...* (Ephesians 1:15-20; see also 3:14-16).

Practice: Close your eyes in prayer and drop down. Yield to Christ within. Think of a favorite Scripture verse. We are told that Christ is the Living Word. Yield to and receive the life of that verse in your heart. The goal is to hold your heart open until you meet the Author of the Word and encounter His mighty presence.

Forgiving

Jesus not only forgave us, but He also instructed us to freely forgive others:

Peter came to Him and said, "Lord, how often shall my brother sin against me, and I forgive him? Up to seven times?" Jesus said to him, "I do not say to you, up to seven times, but up to seventy times seven" (Matthew 18:21-22).

The apostles, likewise, admonished believers to be forgivers, living in the example of Christ forgiving them: *"Be kind to one another, tenderhearted, forgiving one another, even as God in Christ forgave you"* (Eph. 4:32).

Resisting

Resisting is our God-tool that allows us to resist the enemy and hold our spiritual ground. It is a product of our spirit, not that of our willpower. When we resist, we perceive the outside pressure but feel the peace of God residing within our heart. We refuse to give in to the pressure. The enemy can't touch the fruit of the Spirit residing deep within us. As Paul reminds us, *"Therefore, put on every piece of God's armor so you will be able to resist the enemy in the time of evil. Then after the battle you will still be standing firm"* (Eph. 6:13 NLT).

God-Tool #2: Forgiveness

Forgiveness is not only one of the facets of prayer, but it is also the second great God-tool in our spiritual arsenal. In the next chapter we will get some practice in forgiving, but it's important to lay a proper foundation here first.

We have already explained the scriptural location of our heart. God created us with a door in our heart that enables us to make a connection with Him in the Spirit. Now let's consider how connecting with God and encountering His forgiveness physiologically works.

It's important to recognize that the brain is virtually unlimited in its potential for processing information. It can form vast numbers of connections, and there are practically no bounds on the amount of information it can process at any given time. However, we are totally unaware of 99.999 percent of what is going on inside our subconscious mind. So dealing with someone's thoughts and memories is like dealing with one grain of sand compared to all the sand on the beach.

Years ago, I discovered that taking long case histories when dealing with patients is usually a waste of time. We can get lots of information but still know nothing about how it's all connected. That's why after years of talking, a therapist often still has no clue about what's really going on inside a client's head. Can you imagine sitting down and trying to chart out every little thing you do, every emotional reaction and ridiculous thought you have, trying to figure out where they all come from and how they all connect? And that is barely skimming the surface of our thoughts.

So what is really going on inside of us? What things are tying us up in knots? What emotional roots are influencing our thoughts and actions? And how are all these things connected?

The point is that we'll never be able to totally figure ourselves out. Even the best counselors, therapists, or psychiatrists could never be able to really figure us out. They can only guess as to what is going on. As Paul said, *"We know in part and we prophesy in part"* (1 Cor. 13:9). And when it comes to understanding what's going on in the mind, we only know a small part.

But God doesn't guess. He knows exactly what the problem is, what caused it, and how to fix it. Look at the contrast between His complete understanding and our minuscule understanding:

*We don't yet see things clearly. We're squinting in
a fog, peering through a mist. But it won't be long
before the weather clears and the sun shines bright!
We'll see it all then, see it all as clearly as God sees
us, knowing Him directly just as He knows us!*
(1 Corinthians 13:12 MSG)

God-Tool #3: Dealing with Thoughts

It is important to pay attention to our thoughts when it comes
to implementing the God-tools. It doesn't matter if a negative
thought comes from us or the devil, if it doesn't sound like something God would say then don't receive it. We might even want to
say aloud, "I renounce that thought." There is an appropriate old
saying you might have heard, "You can't stop a bird from flying
over your head, but don't let it make a nest in your hair." And the
author of Proverbs tells us, *"Like a flitting sparrow, like a flying
swallow, so a curse without cause shall not alight"* (Prov. 26:2).

Our true identity is the new creation—the part of us that
loves God and loves His Word. The new creation always sounds
like a godly voice, and thinks new creation thoughts. Whenever
we detect a thought or voice that does not sound like the new
creation, we don't have to take it. Paul said, *"Therefore, if anyone is
in Christ, he is a new creation; old things have passed away; behold,
all things have become new"* (2 Cor. 5:17).

Two Categories of Thoughts: Simple Distractions versus
Repetitive Thoughts

If a thought is a mild distraction or worry that causes us to
lose our peace, we just renounce it and release it to God. In this
case, we simply take the *"thought captive to the obedience of Christ"*
(2 Cor. 10:5 NASB).

Practice: Close your eyes and get in an attitude of prayer. Think of a thought that distracts you from time to time. What is the emotion attached to the thought? What are some examples:

Thought: _____

_____

_____

Emotion: _____

_____

_____

Let it go by releasing the thought to Christ within; give it to Him until you get peace.

Mental Strongholds

Most of the time, emotional wounds do not have a lie, or mental stronghold, attached to them. When a lie is believed, it blocks the truth from being received. For example, a person might say, "I know the Bible says God loves me, *but*..." If a mental stronghold is blocking the truth, we can say the truth over and over again, quote Scripture verses, and even beg God to remove the stronghold, but it won't be demolished until we deal with the emotion. Truth bounces off the stronghold like water off a stone tower.

If a person has lived with a lie for a long time, they may come to believe it is their identity, it is who they are. Over the years they have accumulated historical "evidence" to confirm this truth. For example, a person may hear the thought, "I am a failure," and argue that it's true because they have failed in the past. To deal with lies or mental strongholds, always start with the negative emotion (see page 216). Lies come in at the time of emotional wounding. The negative emotion is what gives them power, not just the words themselves.

Historical evidence does not make something scriptural, however. Everyone fails from time to time but it doesn't make them a failure. We can *fail*, but that doesn't make us a *failure*. Labeling a person as a "failure" may be accurate when based on past performance, but the scriptural *fact* is that God never created anyone with a "failure" identity. History is not fact or truth. God and His Word are fact.

Here are some examples of lies based on historical evidence:

- "I am damaged goods."

- "I never do anything right."

- "I never belong."

- "I am unlovable."

- "I am not worthy."

But what does God say about all of these?

What Dennis and I are teaching throughout this book has the potential to save us a lot of time, effort, and therapist fees. Why? Because God knows all about each and every one of us. It won't take Him months or years to figure us out; He already sees to the very core of our being. That's why He, and He alone, is able to give us deep relief, and give it to us now. He has already given us the spiritual equipment necessary to live a godly life in Him, emotionally free, completely whole, and healed.

Chapter 13

GOD INSIDE THE LOOP

By Dr. Jen

The End of Our Rope

Paul describes a fierce inner battle to control unsanctified thoughts and actions in his own life, and thus in the life of believers. He said:

> *I've tried everything and nothing helps. I'm at the end of my rope. Is there no one who can do anything for me? Isn't that the real question?*
>
> *The answer, thank God, is that Jesus Christ can and does. He acted to set things right in this life of contradictions where I want to serve God with all my heart and mind, but am pulled by the influence of sin to do something totally different* (Romans 7:24-25 MSG).

Where does this battle come from in the life of a believer? It comes from the subconscious part of us. That's why David asked

God to search him for hidden time bombs so that he wouldn't really blow it later on. He prayed:

> *Investigate my life, O God, find out everything about me; cross-examine and test me, get a clear picture of what I'm about; see for Yourself whether I've done anything wrong—then guide me on the road to eternal life* (Psalm 139:23-24 MSG).

David knew he was incapable of fully knowing himself or changing himself. He even admitted that he didn't know what was in his own heart. He had to simply depend on God to reveal his hidden, unconscious faults.

> *Who can discern his lapses and errors? Clear me from hidden [and unconscious] faults. Keep back Your servant also from presumptuous sins; let them not have dominion over me! Then shall I be blameless, and I shall be innocent and clear of great transgression* (Psalm 19:12-13 AMP).

> *I acknowledged my sin to You, and my iniquity I did not hide. I said, I will confess my transgressions to the Lord [continually unfolding the past till all is told]—then You [instantly] forgave me the guilt and iniquity of my sin. Selah [pause, and calmly think of that]!* (Psalm 32:5 AMP)

When you think of this kind of transparency before God, how does it make you feel? Scared? Hopeful? At peace? The Lord wants us to know that our heart is fully visible to Him—even before we are willing see it. So we may as well be honest with Him. That's the only real path to lasting relief and transformation.

There Is Hope

There have been many people we have ministered to over the years that were at the end of their rope, experiencing contradictions between what they were called to and what they were currently experiencing. By implementing the God-tools, the spiritual equipment He has given to each of us, they were able to experience deep relief and freedom from their emotional pain. And He can do the same for you.

Relief from Post-Traumatic Stress Injury (PTSI)

An Episcopal priest had been serving in the Navy reserves and was called up for active duty as a chaplain. Dennis and I had taught the God-tools at his church a few years prior, and he began to use the how-tos in his own life and ministry. He was amazed by the fast and effective results he saw. But now, as a chaplain, he had to counsel wounded war veterans diagnosed with post-traumatic stress injury (PTSI). When they came to his office, he used the God-tools and got such good results that the Navy physicians and psychiatrists soon took notice of what he was doing. There is hope.

A Pastor's Job Gets Easier

Some time ago we spent several days teaching at a church, and the pastor asked if we would pray for some of his parishioners. We scheduled short appointments, used the God-tools, and people were quickly healed and set free as we prayed with them.

The pastor watched from a distance and said afterward, "This was amazing! It was so fast, and it worked amazingly well." He saw that our approach was much different than the "therapeutic model" used by most counselors: "You didn't sit there listening to them vent and complain. You just prayed through a few things, and they were healed!"

The pastor also noticed that instead of focusing on ourselves, we had taught his parishioners how to use the DRN principles for *themselves*. "I have been doing ministry the hard way," he said. "This is the way I am going to do my appointments from now on. You just made my job a lot easier!" There is hope when we're at the end of our rope.

It's No Longer Hard to Receive

Dennis and I traveled to a church as members of a ministry team, and after the sermon was done, we were all asked to minister to the congregation at an altar call. The microphone was handed to Dennis, and he gave a special invitation for people to come to the altar for prayer. He said, "I want to pray for those of you who feel unspiritual or have been judged by others as 'hard to receive' the things of God." A man commented under his breath, "You'd never catch me asking for that. The results could be pretty embarrassing."

Many responded, and Dennis taught them the how-tos on receiving from God. The Lord powerfully touched every single one of them, some for the first time in their lives. As they encountered the presence of God, inner conflict and frustration suddenly disappeared—and it happened instantly. There was hope for them, and there is hope for you and me.

Surprised By God's Presence and Love

A pastor's wife in Connecticut was attending one of our training seminars not long ago. We taught on how to use the God-tools in prayer. She thought, "Okay, I'll give this a try." All of a sudden, she felt a powerful sense of the love and presence of God. It surprised her so much that she stopped praying and opened her eyes. "Wow!" she wondered. "What just happened?" She closed her eyes and tried it again, immediately sensing God's presence.

Later, she told us the God-tools changed her prayer life forever. They opened up a whole new dimension in her relationship with God and were tremendously useful for everyday life. Even though she had been a believer for years, God showed up and renewed hope within her.

The Original Desperate Housewife

A New England housewife joked that she had been the *original* desperate housewife. She had been at the end of her rope, but God showed up. She wrote to us, "Before I met the Clarks, I had so much fear. Even though I had been born again decades before, my overwhelming fear sometimes resulted in panic attacks and out-of-control thoughts and feelings. I expended all my energy each day in planning to stay 'on top of things.'

"I constantly wanted attention, tried to be (and do) whatever pleased other people, was defensive when confronted, and shut myself off from other people and life in general. Mood swings ranged from high to low with angry explosive behavior in between. On top of all that, I struggled with feelings of incompetence and a fear of failure. I lived in condemnation and shame.

"Dennis and Dr. Jen taught me how to use the God-tools in my life, and I was able to deal with the baggage of the past. Now I practice the how-tos daily. My story is much like Dr. Jen's story, because I have been transformed too. Now I truly sense that God is with me. I feel protected and no longer have to put up walls. I am finally free to enjoy and accept others, and I'm free to be myself in God.

"Because of what I've learned, I know how to open to life and people. Instead of feeling insecure and intimidated, I am more consistently stable and 'rooted.' My internal conflict has been turned into inner peace." There is hope for us when we're at the end of our rope.

Our Gut Is Our Second Brain

Have you ever received bad news and feel like you had been punched in the gut? Some people even have trouble swallowing—or swallow too often—when the nerves in their esophagus are highly stimulated. Have you ever gotten emotional about something and felt like you had a "lump in your throat"?

During early embryonic development, the neural crest splits into two parts, half of which migrates to the head to form the brain and central nervous system (CNS). The other half migrates to the gut, and lines the intestines, stomach, and esophagus, forming the enteric nervous system (ENS). Our gastrointestinal tract has been called the "second brain," because it contains as many nerve cells as the brain and central nervous system.

The emotional center of the brain, the limbic system, relays emotional information directly to the intestines by way of the left vagus nerve, and the gut transmits emotional information back to the brain through releasing neuropeptides, the molecules of emotion. This is why our digestive tract is so sensitive to emotions.

This is why many of us have experienced an upset stomach when our emotions were upset. For example, fear stimulates the vagus nerve to turn up the volume on serotonin circuits in the gut. Serotonin is a molecule of emotion that also helps regulate intestinal activity. When the gut is overstimulated by serotonin, intestinal spasms, pain, or even diarrhea may occur.

Emotions Inform Our Body

Suppose we are alone in a quiet house, and we suddenly hear a loud crash. Immediately we feel startled, and we physically feel the emotion of fear. Our heart beats faster, our muscles tense, the pupils of our eyes dilate, and stress hormone levels increase. Then our thoughts catch up to the emotion, and we realize that the dog simply knocked over a mop that was leaning against the wall. The fear leaves, and our body returns to its normal state.

Emotions are activated before thoughts. Incoming information goes to the brain's relay center, the thalamus, which operates like an air traffic control center. Signals are sent to both our emotional center and our thought center at the same time. However, our emotions form before our thinking can catch up with the emotional reaction. Our whole body experiences the emotion before our brain creates a thought, because each additional neural pathway adds a few more milliseconds. It takes longer for our brain to sort through all the memories, associations, and perceptions of a lifetime than it takes for an emotion to be triggered.

It's crucial to realize that our whole body receives emotional information. Emotions are like the intercom of the body, the communication system. When an emotion is generated in the brain (even before conscious thought can form), a cascade of neuropeptides, or "nerve proteins," are released to send the message to every cell in our body. This is why it is so important that we receive emotional healing.

Our Biography Becomes Our Biology

Cell membranes have surface receptors that detect and respond to environmental signals, including emotional communication. When these molecules of emotion fit into cellular receptors on the outside surface of each cell, the information is transmitted to the interior of the cell and begins to change the inside. This process has been described as a key fitting into a keyhole. Emotional information is stored in the cellular memory. We might not have realized it before, but our emotions are stored in our cells.

The surface of each one of our cells has identity receptors, which actually contain our entire life story. They tell what our life has been like and who we are now. There is an old saying about people who let their emotions show easily, "Their heart is written on their sleeve." Actually, it would be more accurate to say, "Our heart is written on our cells." When our heart, our inner being, changes, our cells change too. Who we become is imprinted on our very cells.

God created us with the physical capacity to be transformed in the cells of our body. When we were born again, we became a new creation spiritually, and the "new creation" was inscribed on every cell. As we spend time in prayer and grow in the grace and the knowledge of God, our cells reflect it. When God's love touches our heart, it transforms us spiritually and physically. Change inside becomes change outside. Paul reminded the Thessalonians of this very thing: *"Now may the God of peace Himself sanctify you completely; and may your whole spirit, soul, and body be preserved blameless at the coming of our Lord Jesus Christ"* (1 Thess. 5:23).

Throughout our lifetime, whatever we tell our cells through our emotions is actually written in our cells' memory. Amazing as it may seem, through our emotions we can speak either health or disease directly to our cells. Whether we have healthy emotions or toxic emotions, our biography becomes our biology.

This fact points to the big problem with traditional counseling methods: our emotions are much more powerful than our thoughts. Emotions control both our thinking and our choices—and this isn't something a therapist can just talk us out of.

Joseph LeDoux, author of *The Emotional Brain*, says the aim of psychoanalysis is for the thoughts (cortex) to gain control of the emotions. But he admits this is a difficult and prolonged process.[1]

So is it possible the thoughts aren't the best place to start, after all? Is there a way healing and relief can originate with the emotions instead?

Making the Connection: The Feeling-Thought Loop

How does this connection work in relation to prayer and forgiveness? When we open the door of our heart in prayer, the love of God can flow into our entire being. If the door of our heart is already open to God, all we have to do in order to be forgiven is yield to His forgiveness.

Have you ever heard of something called a feedback loop? One example of a feedback loop is when the pancreas increases the production of insulin after we eat. If blood sugar levels rise, the endocrine system triggers insulin production in the pancreas to counteract the increase and return blood sugar levels to normal. At this point, the pancreas is signaled to stop producing and releasing the insulin within our body. It is a closed unit that operates automatically.

Each one of us has a feeling-thought feedback loop that intricately connects our head, heart, organs, and systems. You see, emotions cannot be divided from thoughts. Because the brain automatically links our thoughts and emotions together—it's impossible to separate them. They are inextricably joined as feeling-thought units, which are also known as emo-cognition feedback loops.

The Bible shows this clear interweaving of our heart, our emotions, our thoughts, and our hurtful ways. Again, looking at the way David prayed shows how all of these are intricately connected. He said, *"Search me, O God, and know my heart; try me and know my anxious thoughts; and see if there be any hurtful way in me, and lead me in the everlasting way"* (Ps. 139:23-24 NASB).

Our brain combines thought and emotion into indivisible units. When an event is stored in the brain's long-term memory, it's saved as a feeling-thought entity, merged within the loop. Our mind and body operate as one system, which explains some of what Paul was struggling with in Romans 7. Because the activity in the feedback loop is beyond our control, it keeps on operating the same way despite our attempts to change.

When someone refers to something as pushing their buttons, their feeling-thought loop has been triggered, bringing a negative emotion to the surface. Every time that button is pushed, they react automatically and negatively. This can make it hard for people to change when it comes to their feeling-thoughts. It is not impossible, but just hard.

Not only is there an emo-cognition loop, but there is also an emo-volition loop. According to Jonathan Edwards, our will and our affections are so closely intertwined that they operate as one indivisible unit.[2] He writes in *A Treatise Concerning Religious Affections,* "The will and affections of the soul are not two faculties; the affections are not essentially distinct from the will, nor do they differ from mere actings of the will, and inclination of the soul, but only in the liveliness and sensibleness of exercise."[3] He went on to describe two categories of emotion we all possess—affections and passions. He was essentially differentiating between the fruit of the Spirit and our carnal emotions.[4]

All of this doesn't mean it's impossible for change to occur in either our emo-cognition loop or within the emo-volition loop. However, it takes something from the outside breaking into the loop to change the dynamics within the system. Otherwise, the same cycle just keeps repeating itself.

Getting God in the Loop

The most common approach in traditional therapy has been attempting to force a person's thinking to control their emotions. Counselors and psychotherapists try to bring about transformation by breaking into the feeling-thought feedback loop. But this is much harder than it sounds. And counselors admit that if they can't modify what is going on inside the loop, the person will be unable to change.

Both Christian and secular counselors attempt to get into the feedback loop and bring internal change in people's thoughts, emotions, and choices. However, while almost all approaches try to change the thoughts to get to the emotions, this rarely works.

Perhaps the following analogy will help illustrate the different approaches to finding transformation and relief from emotional pain. If I wanted to get inside my house, I could drag a ladder around to the kitchen window, climb up the ladder, force the window open, and try to crawl through the window without knocking the ladder over. Or if I decided it was too hard to break in that way, I could just give up and pitch a tent in the yard instead. Sadly, many believers just give up and camp outside of God's best for them.

Certainly, God doesn't want us to give up. But how can we get in the "house"? Wouldn't it be easier to just unlock the front door and step right inside? It would definitely require less time and effort. In the same way, it's really hard to get into the feeling-thought feedback loop without going through the door. And it becomes "a difficult and prolonged task," as Joseph LeDoux admits.

God Has a Better Way

We don't need a ladder or a burglar's kit to break into the loop. As we have already seen, God has designed a special door that provides access into the loop. Jesus reminds us:

> *Most assuredly, I say to you, he who does not enter the sheepfold by the door, but climbs up some other way, the same is a thief and a robber. But he who enters by the door is the shepherd of the sheep* (John 10:1-2).

The Bible says this door is in the heart, the seat of our emotions. That's why lasting transformation must begin in the heart, and why it always involves the emotions. The good news is that if we connect with God through prayer, we have let Him in the loop. After that, things that were very hard for us to do by ourselves will become easy through the power of God and the empowerment of His grace.

If prayer begins with an open heart, then forgiveness must also start with the heart. And this means forgiveness starts with our emotions as well as with our thoughts and choices. As soon as God is in the loop, He can forgive through us. Christ the forgiver lives inside each of us. So we have to stop "trying" to forgive and simply yield to Christ the forgiver in our heart, allowing Him to forgive through us. That is the secret to using our prayer and forgiveness God-tools.

ENDNOTES

1. J. LeDoux, *The Emotional Brain: The Mysterious Underpinnings of Emotional Life* (New York: Simon and Schuster, 1996), 303.
2. Jonathan Edwards, *A Treatise Concerning Religious Affections* (New York: Cosimo Classics, 2007), 9,24.
3. Ibid., 10,25.
4. Ibid., 11,26.

Chapter 14

FORGIVE 1-2-3

By Dr. Jen

Committed to DRN

When doors began opening for Dennis and me to minister in churches and conferences in 1998, we wanted to develop the best and quickest ways to teach people how to deal with painful emotional issues. Dennis had been using these principles in his own life and ministry for years, but they hadn't yet been known as deep relief now.

I was still new at all of this, so I constantly reflected back on the steps Dennis had taken to teach the principles to me. In 1999 we were asked to teach at a school of ministry in West Haven, Connecticut, one night a week for four months. That meant staying in New England from January to the beginning of May. As soon as we committed to do that, other ministry schools, churches, prayer groups, and even a couple of businesses with Christian owners asked us to train their people as well. So we worked on training manuals, made sets of some audio teachings, planned out a curriculum, and began to develop instruction methods.

Although the basic DRN approach has a 100 percent success rate in bringing people deep relief (unless they refuse to forgive), some trial and error was needed to develop and hone our terminology and teaching materials. Over the next few years, we saw where improvement was needed, what required clarification, and what should be added. We even wrote a troubleshooting manual for prayer teams so they would know how to get past any temporary obstacles that arose while in prayer sessions.

This period of time proved to be foundational to the rest of our ministry. Our objective all along was simple: to provide a clear and practical biblical methodology for people to experience deep relief from their own pain and then be equipped to help others too. Yes, we wanted to bless people with a knowledge of the inner healing and restoration available to them in Christ, but we also wanted to equip them to be a blessing to others through the principles they learned from us (see Gen. 12:2).

From the beginning, our passion has been to teach people everything we know, in effect working ourselves out of a job. For our first training classes in New England, we gave people a prayer card "cheat sheet" so they could use it in ministering to their fellow classmates. It was thrilling to see everyone in the room, cards in hand, successfully praying with each other to bring deep relief to their deepest wounds.

Simple Enough for a Child

A young mother who was bubbling over with excitement once approached me. She rushed up to me at the beginning of class and shared that a bitter divorce had left her and her two young sons very wounded. But she had used the prayer card to lead her sons, ages 7 and 10, in forgiving their father. "Right before my eyes," she told me, "I saw a visible change in my sons' countenances as their pain left. They've been amazingly different since I prayed with them. And now the ten-year-old is even helping other children pray through their heart woundings."

This young mom's story really inspired me. Somehow even back then, we had simplified the process so much so that both adults and children could use it in their own healing and in helping others.

When one person or married couple receives deep relief, it benefits them personally. But there is also a ripple effect that extends to the next generation. This ignited a brand-new dream in my heart. Wouldn't it be wonderful if parents, schoolteachers, and everyone who ministers to teens and children could impart these principles? I could envision an entire generation of young people in the church who could grow up without the burden of painful emotional baggage, be emotionally healthy spouses who wouldn't destroy their marriages, and become parents who didn't pass along toxic emotions and destructive behavior patterns to the next generation.

First-Feel-Forgive

This chapter came out of a two-session retreat I did for some hurting women in a rustic setting some time ago. I was there with two goals in mind: to bring deep relief to these women's hearts and to provide them with tools they could take with them to help others.

During the evening session, I taught for a while, then offered to minister for as long as anyone still wanted prayer. There were lots of tears, then lots of healing, joy, and freedom that night.

For the morning session, I prayed, "Lord, how can I give them something simpler, more effective, and easier to remember than what Dennis and I have used before?" The principles were clearly bringing deep relief and transformation, but I wanted to make sure they were packaged in such a simple way that people could continue using them in their daily lives.

Quickly responding to my prayer, the Lord gave me three words: first, feel, forgive. I immediately realized that these three words were a shorthand version of the steps and sequence of prayer we had been following. And I saw that the body of Christ could be radically healed if believers knew and applied only these three simple steps: first-feel-forgive.

Forgive 1-2-3

These are the three simple steps to healing, or as we refer to it, forgive 1-2-3. If we follow this 1-2-3 process, our longstanding emotional pain can be healed quickly and completely—no person is too damaged, no pain is too great. You see, the DRN principles aren't just a nice theory. They really work. I've seen countless transformations, beginning with my own story, and in the lives of many, many others.

An Example from My Own Life

I originally had a horrible fear of public speaking. During graduate school, I could hardly even do an oral presentation. Despite having a great desire to teach, I would get so scared that my skin would feel cold and clammy. And as I started to speak, I would freeze up and stumble over my words, forgetting what I wanted to say.

Dennis and I had been married almost a year when he was asked to do a seminar at a local church. Let me be clear: Dennis was going to do a seminar, and I was going to just listen to him teach. Two days before the seminar, however, Dennis suggested I should do half of the teachings.

My mouth dropped open as I exclaimed, "I can't do that, Dennis! I would have to pray and prepare at least twenty hours to be able to stand up in front of a crowd and speak. Since I don't have time to do that, there's no way I can help teach the seminar."

Patiently but firmly he replied, "You know the material really well, and it's not normal to be so afraid to speak when you have so much to share. Sit down and let's pray right now to get to the root of that."

Dennis then asked me, "Who is the first person or situation that comes to your mind?" As soon as I closed my eyes in prayer, I saw myself as a little girl in first grade. However, my first thought was, "That's so silly. What does that have to do with anything?"

I remembered leaving the school playground at recess and coming into the building to use the restroom. But I got lost in the halls, couldn't find the restroom, and then couldn't find my way back outside to get help from my teacher. As I described this scene to Dennis, he told me to let myself feel the emotion attached to my memories. Much to my surprise, I felt fear in my gut, almost to the point of panic.

Prior to this, I had absolutely no idea any fear from that situation was still residing in my heart. If another person had frightened me, I would have needed to forgive them. But in this case, there was no one to forgive. I had caused the situation all by myself. So Dennis told me to receive forgiveness for allowing that fear to come in. And as soon as I yielded to forgiveness from Christ the forgiver in me, the fear left and I instantly felt peace.

You may be asking at this point, "What does any of this have to do with your fear of teaching, Dr. Jen?" Well, two days later I taught my half of the seminar without any fear, and I haven't stopped teaching since. Now I absolutely love teaching. I don't get even the least bit nervous. But how amazing it was that a so-called "little thing," which occurred many years ago, had been blocking a major part of God's plan for my life.

Experiences like this taught me to quickly deal with whatever issues God brings up. The Lord is really smart, and He can see things in my heart that I'm unable to see yet. I saw that all my psychological analysis is of no consequence compared to the wisdom of God.

Our Marriage Was Transformed

Some time ago we met a couple only a few months after they were married. They had some serious emotional issues and clashes that wouldn't go away. They described themselves as "desperate." Even though they loved each other deeply, they couldn't seem to stop triggering each other's inner wounds.

"After being mentored by Dennis and Jen," they wrote, "we learned how to work through the first-feel-forgive exercises. They challenged us to focus on old memories instead of the current troubles we were having with each other. We did what they said, and we started seeing results the very first night." The process was beginning to work for them.

After going through the process for some time, they began to experience supernatural transformation in their hearts and it overflowed into their marriage. "Because of emotional healing and growth, we were able to relate to each other and understand each other much better," they said. "With the simple tools we received, we were finally able to establish a firm foundation for our marriage. Our relationship has truly been transformed."

Try It Yourself

So how does first-feel-forgive work in practice? Here's an outline of how you can try it now for yourself. As we close our eyes and pray, we yield to Christ in our heart. We are opening our heart to Him so He can reveal any areas that need to be sanctified through prayer and forgiveness.

First: Focus on the first person or situation that comes to mind.

What is the first real person or memory that you think of? Don't dismiss it if it seems insignificant or you don't understand why you thought of it. God knows the order to go in, and sometimes the issues that seem small to us have tremendous significance in our lives. After I experienced that healing from the fear I experienced when getting lost in first grade, I learned to just go with whatever comes to mind.

Feel: Feel the negative emotion that you felt when the situation occurred.

You only have to feel the negative emotion momentarily, but when you allow the Lord to cleanse the pain, your reward will be a lifetime of peace in that area. Pay attention to how the emotion feels inside of you. It has been residing in you ever since the event happened, even if it's been hiding beneath the surface of your conscious thoughts most of the time.

Remember that unresolved emotions are stored in your brain's long-term memory and in the cellular memory of your entire body. But God can heal these once they are brought to the light. As you present your heart to Him for transformation, He not only reveals but He also heals.

Forgive: Let a river of forgiveness flow until the negative emotion changes to peace.

Yield to Christ the forgiver who lives within you. He is the One who does the forgiving. Forgiveness may be directed either toward God, yourself, or other people. Sometimes you will have to forgive in more than one direction, or sometimes in all three directions.

For example, a person who was molested might be angry at the perpetrator, blame themselves for not stopping it somehow, and feel hurt and disappointed with God because it was allowed to happen. When in doubt, forgive in all three directions, because you can't forgive too much. You'll know your forgiveness is complete when the negative emotion is replaced with a feeling of deep peace inside.

Keys for Healing Prayer

It's important to review the keys we've discussed about simple prayer and forgiveness. Dennis learned these principles during his over 35 years of experience in ministry, but they are much different from anything I was ever taught in my training as a Christian counselor.

As a starting point, we must remember that Jesus never refuses anyone who wants to be saved (see Rom. 10:13). We simply just have to invite Him into our heart and confess with our mouth, and then we're saved. In exactly the same way, Jesus never refuses to heal a heart of pain. All we have to do is expose the pain to Him and allow His forgiveness to wash away any toxic emotions. As we received Him into our heart for salvation, we must live in Him by continually keeping our heart's door open to His loving, healing presence. Again, Paul reminds us, *"So then, just as you received Christ Jesus as Lord, continue to live in Him"* (Col. 2:6 NIV).

As we practice healing prayer in our own life and in helping others, there are a few important points to remember: Christ is the forgiver, so forgiveness works every time; forgiveness is instantaneous, not a process; and there is no "big" or "little" problem in God's sight—it's all easy for Him.

Practice: Before reading any further, I encourage you to take a few minutes to practice what you've just learned about first-feel-forgive.

- Sequence is important, so always go in God's order as you pray.

- Pray through one thing at a time until you get peace in that area.

The DRN approach always works for a person who truly wants help. It is faster than other approaches because it gets God into the feeling-thought loop more quickly and efficiently. Transformation occurs when God touches the heart and heals negative emotions and inner wounds that may have caused distress for years.

Some More Stories

Assurance of Her Salvation

A young woman scheduled an appointment for prayer with Dennis and me. But when we began to pray with her, she said her main problem was that she wasn't sure she was actually saved. She went on to explain that although she regularly answered altar calls for salvation, she was never really assured where she stood with God. As a result, she continually wrestled with tormenting doubts. Over the years, a number of people had tried to help and encourage her, yet the questions in her head could never be silenced.

We asked her to close her eyes and pray with us, and we taught her how to hear God's voice. At last, she could hear the Lord clearly and receive settled assurance that she was His child. She wept tears of joy as she finally received a deep sense of God's acceptance. She told us later she was now able to enjoy intimacy with God for the very first time. And all because she learned to deal with the doubts in her heart, allowing Christ to come and assure her of His precious gift.

Living from His Peace Within

A missionary to Belize, Central America, wrote to us a couple of years ago, telling us about a transformation that occurred deep within. He wrote, "Dennis Clark...was my mentor in living from His peace within. Before I met Dennis, I often felt the Holy Spirit come on me, but not remain. Of course I believed He lived in me by faith. But Dennis showed me how to stay in touch with the Spirit within. The inner walls that block our experience of the Holy Spirit are simply unforgiveness, doubts, and unconfessed sin."

Dennis said to him while ministering to him, "Now let Christ in you go to that wall, and through that wall." Suddenly a rush of love flowed out of him and washed away all traces of hurt and hesitation. He said, "It was so liberating that I eagerly did the same with everyone I could think of—including myself. As I released every pain to Christ within, His peace flowed to places that bitter roots had clutched, till the peace that passes understanding filled me."

Dennis then reminded him to live from that place of peace. "Whenever anything disrupts your peace, submit it to Christ within. Any feelings of hurt, fear, lust, anger, or guilt are toxic emotions that can be cleansed by His blood, if you confess and give them to Him." And that is what he has been doing since that time, experiencing the peace of Christ in ever-greater ways.

Stopped By a Policeman

Stina had been to some of our seminars, and she had already learned how to deal with toxic emotions and find relief and peace. One day she was driving behind a truck that drove right through a red light. Stina didn't notice that the light was red and just followed the other vehicle in front of her.

A policeman standing on the corner didn't see the truck, but he saw Stina. He pulled her over and was yelling at her as he walked toward her car. Stina was so shaken emotionally that her hands were trembling. In the midst of this stressful situation, the thought came to her, "I've got to remember what Dennis and Dr. Jen taught me: 'Drop down and go to Christ within.'" Her hands immediately stopped shaking. "Hey, that really worked!" she realized. She then got even bolder, allowing a river of loving forgiveness to flow toward the policeman.

By the time he got to her car window, he wasn't yelling anymore. He paused and said, "Oh, lady, I hate going to court. Just go on now." The moral of the story is not how to get out of a traffic ticket, but that when we yield to Christ, He's able to change us and also the atmosphere around us. We can experience deep relief now, and our whole life can be changed as we live from a place of peace.

One Last Story

I want to share a very dramatic story, and I must say that I have never seen the Lord deal with so many significant traumas all at one time before. So I am glad that we had a roomful of witnesses during this particular prayer session.

Dennis and I were driving with a group of pastors in Canada, and were in transit somewhere between two different provinces. It was quite a long distance, so we stopped to spend the night halfway, where we had been asked to have dinner and participate in a small house meeting afterward.

After the meeting was underway, a Micmac Indian woman suddenly had an emotional meltdown, wailing, "It's so much. My whole life, I want more of God, but my whole life, it's just too much! You don't understand!"

Well, the other pastors in the room immediately called us over. Dennis said to her, "Just calm down, it's okay. We are going to go through just one thing at a time. It is all right. Now, just one at a time. People may not understand, but Jesus understands. What is the first person or situation that you see? Just stay focused on the first one that comes to mind. As soon as you get peace on that one, we'll deal with the next."

Dennis and I then prayed her through five major traumas: being physically beaten as a child, sexual molestation, having three abortions, rape, and seeing her son murdered right before her eyes on the reservation. We led her through prayer, and she experienced peace each time before going any further. In under 20 minutes, she was not only at peace, but she was actually joyful to be experiencing so much freedom.

Then she said, "Teach me how to do this. Explain to me what you did because I have to take this with me. I want to know how to help all those other hurting people on the reservation." So we gave her a mini-class right then and there. She left the meeting later with a glow on her face and a package of how-to training materials in her hand. There is nothing that can compare to the joy of helping people who are ignited with a passion to bring healing to others.

These champions for the Lord are storm chasers, because they are equipped and fervent to proclaim the good news of peace to the hearts of wounded souls. They don't run from the storms, they run to them:

> *How beautiful upon the mountains are the feet of him who brings good news, who proclaims peace, who*

brings glad tidings of good things, who proclaims salvation, who says to Zion, "Your God reigns!" (Isaiah 52:7)

So now you have the basic tools needed for receiving deep relief now. Are you ready for a transformed life—and a life that can bring transformation to others as well?

Conclusion

READY TO RECEIVE DEEP RELIEF NOW?

By Dennis

Do you want to be healed—emotionally, spiritually, and physically? If you do, then we have resources available for you. Even though I'm sure you answered that question in the affirmative, surprisingly enough, not everyone does. Jesus addressed this issue when He asked the man who had a spirit of infirmity, "Wilt thou be made whole?" (see John 5:5-7 KJV).

This book has contained many testimonies throughout of what the Lord can do in your own life, thus increasing your faith. And there are a few more contained in the Appendix: More Testimonies. Pray for yourself, using the first-feel-forgive model. After you experience the power of God working in your own life through these simple steps, show this book to others who need DRN and healing prayer as well.

You can also visit our websites, www.Forgive123.com and www.DeepReliefNow.com, for additional resources and information. We have an online store on each of the sites with books and materials designed to teach the how-tos of deep relief now and how to connect with God in deep and intimate ways.

The Simple Prayer DVD and CD set also functions as a healing prayer personal trainer. In this set I coach you through the steps, so you pray through the DRN steps with the Healing Prayer CD as your guide.

This book only covers the basics of what Jen and I teach everywhere we go. If you want to delve deeper, we have instruction on how to deal with thoughts and mental strongholds, generational sin, sexual issues, the impact of prayer on cellular biology and physical healing, and much, much more.

Do you feel that you're called to become a minister of DRN and want to train others? We have developed a boot camp of practical training, a course of intensive study, through TEAM Embassy.

The DRN basic tool is a blue three-by-five card called, appropriately enough, the Blue Card, which is small enough to keep in your pocket for reference. Why is it blue? Because blue is the color of revelation. It outlines the first-feel-forgive steps, with two additional steps that are only occasionally needed. If you mastered only the Blue Card, you could become healed and whole in a very short period of time.

Suppose you had 100 serious traumas (though we have never met anyone who had that much damage—that would seem overwhelming to most people), and you used the Blue Card to pray through just one a day, it would only take three months and ten days to pray through them all. And if you prayed through three a day, it would just take a few days over a month. How does that compare to years of traditional counseling?

What if you then took the Blue Card and taught these steps to others? You could have healed friends and family members (if they want to be healed). Whole church congregations could be healed. Children could learn these simple steps and not grow up with all the baggage that ruins lives, destroys marriages, and wounds their own offspring, passing the damage along to the next generation. We have prototype churches where the pastors testify, "We have a healthy church thanks to DRN!"

The principles of the Blue Card are simply a description of the way I observed the Holy Spirit working during prayer sessions. Again, it is not a method, but this is the way the Lord moved to first bring healing into my own life, and then how the Holy Spirit later touched the lives of others over the years. I simply followed the leading of the Holy Spirit. Now I can see God's wisdom in the pattern He revealed to me.

Several years after Jen and I were married, the Lord gave revelation of a shorthand way to help people remember the simple DRN steps. It started with first, feel, forgive, and then we later added two more steps, fact and fill. (However, most of the time a person will need only steps 1-2-3.) Make the Blue Card and the DRN steps part of your daily life and share what you have learned with others.

> We use our powerful God-tools for...fitting every loose thought and emotion and impulse into the structure of life shaped by Christ. Our tools are ready at hand for clearing the ground of every obstruction and building lives of obedience into maturity (2 Corinthians 10:5 MSG).

Blue Card Prayer: Minister under the Umbrella of Prayer

Close Your Eyes and Pray

- -

First: What is the first person or situation that comes to mind?

Feel: Allow yourself to feel the emotion.

Forgive: Let Christ the forgiver forgive through you. Allow a river of forgiveness to flow through the negative emotion until it changes to peace. (Forgiveness may be toward God, self, or others.)

Fact: Most emotional wounds do not have a lie attached. But occasionally a lie may be believed at the time of an emotional wounding and become a mental stronghold. Let forgiveness flow first until you have peace, then:

1. **Renounce:** renounce the lie out loud.
2. **Replace:** ask the Holy Spirit to tell you the truth (fact).
3. **Receive:** allow it to be written on your heart.

Fill: Then, if there was an emotional need that wasn't met, such as love or attention, forgive first, then release (use the God-tool of releasing) demands on people, and receive filling from the Holy Spirit.

- -

Appendix

MORE TESTIMONIES

Living in Fear and Rejection

"My life used to be lived in fear and rejection most of the time. But the healing I've received through the deep relief now approach has enabled me to experience being loved and wanted by God. Now I don't fear people's rejection anymore. I have a deep contentment and satisfaction in knowing I am loved by God."

Impure Thoughts

"Although I'm a pastor, I used to struggle with impure thoughts. At times my thoughts would be carried away with things that were embarrassing and shameful. I tried to use God's Word to quiet these thoughts, but it still was a constant battle. This made me feel very ashamed and unworthy of God's love. However, with the help of Dennis and Dr. Jen, my deep emotional wounds were healed within half an hour. How amazing, that within a half hour I was free of the shameful thoughts that had tormented me for years."

Something Missing from My Life

"As a pastor, I told my congregation that God is real. Yet even though I talked about God and read about God, something was missing from my life. I concluded that if I couldn't *feel* God and truly see something happen, the rest of the stuff didn't really mean much to me. I used to go to Christian counselors and sit on the couch and talk about my issues and problems. But often I left even more upset, because I had simply churned up all my pain. The problems just couldn't be fixed. But with the DRN approach of Dennis and Dr. Jen, everything changed. You can feel the transformation, and there's proof in your life."

A Higher Spiritual Level

"Dennis Clark mentored me in my relationship with the Lord and helped me return to the mission field at a higher spiritual level than I had known before. I learned how to live from Christ in my heart, not just from my mind. I'm particularly grateful that I've learned how to totally forgive from Christ in my heart. Jesus has fulfilled His promise in John 8:36, and I am now 'free indeed.'"

A Basket Case

"The Lord used DRN to change my life. It has been an amazing deliverance for me to operate in the principles of God's peace being *the* umpire of every situation in my life. I would have been a basket case if I hadn't been taught the 'drop down' principles from Dennis and Dr. Jen. I don't think there's anything more critical in the life of a believer than these principles you've so faithfully taught me."

Nightmares Are Gone

"After I was in a horrible car wreck, I was afraid all the time. I couldn't drive my car without feeling panicky, and I had ongoing nightmares. Yet I was completely healed in just one prayer session. I have no more nightmares, no more dread, and no more problems with driving a car."

ABOUT THE CLARKS

Dennis and Dr. Jen equip believers to heal themselves, then to facilitate healing to others. It is not counseling in the traditional sense, but a brand- new approach, teaching believers how to experience the peace of God in everyday life, and how to deal quickly and completely with anything interrupting their peace. Some individuals may just want to receive quick healing for a few wounds and traumas, but many others have become committed to making peace a way of life, like the Clarks have learned to do.

They have spent years developing teaching materials based on spiritual revelation that has now been developed into targeted training modules which can be tailored for mature believers, new converts, Sunday school teachers, youth pastors, church discipleship programs, pastoral care, restoration, ministry teams, missionaries, and lay workers. The simple keys are easy enough for a mother or Sunday school worker to teach a 3-year-old child, yet effective enough to heal the deepest hurts of adults quickly and completely. Advanced topics are also taught in other training seminars: dealing with the thought life, emotional health, willpower, addiction, deliverance, sexual issues, physical healing, and spiritual discernment.

Dennis and Dr. Jen are the authors of *Live Free: Discover the Keys to Living in God's Presence 24/7*, *Deep Relief Now: Simple*

Keys for Quickly Healing Your Longstanding Emotional Pain. In addition, they have a series for children, *The Great God Quest,* that teaches the how-tos to children. Dr Jen is also author of *Was Jesus a Capitalist?*

clark@forgive123.com

www.forgive123.com

LIVE *FREE*

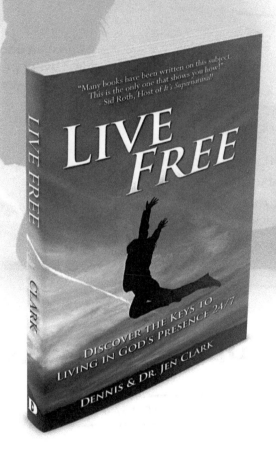

If you missed Dennis & Dr. Jen's first book
Live Free, you can pick up your copy at
www.forgive123.com, or wherever books are sold.

FREE E-BOOKS?
YES, PLEASE!

Get **FREE** and deeply-discounted **Christian books** for your **e-reader** delivered to your inbox **every week!**

IT'S SIMPLE!

VISIT lovetoreadclub.com

SUBSCRIBE by entering your email address

RECEIVE free and discounted e-book offers and inspiring articles delivered to your inbox every week!

Unsubscribe at any time.

SUBSCRIBE NOW!

LOVE TO READ CLUB

visit **LOVETOREADCLUB.COM** ▶